L RMS USITANIA

The Ship & Her Record

ERIC SAUDER

TEMPUS

Front cover illustration: Dated 1907, this watercolor by C.E. Turner shows *Lusitania* in Liverpool around the time of her maiden voyage. In the background is an earlier Cunarder, and off *Lusitania*'s starboard bow is the tender *Skirmisher* of 1884. (Original painting, author's collection)

Frontispiece: A sketch of *Lusitania* on her speed trials. (Original sketch by Ken Marschall, author's collection)

First published 2005

Tempus Publishing Limited
The Mill, Brimscombe Port,
Stroud, Gloucestershire, GL5 2QG
www.tempus-publishing.com

© Eric Sauder, 2005

The right of Eric Sauder to be identified as the Author
of this work has been asserted in accordance with the
Copyrights, Designs and Patents Act 1988.

British Library Cataloguing in Publication Data.
A catalogue record for this book is available from the British Library.

ISBN 0 7524 3417 9

Typesetting and origination by Tempus Publishing Limited.
Printed in Great Britain.

CONTENTS

FOREWORD

Olympic. Mauretania. Queen Mary. Bremen. France. United States. For decades I was fortunate enough to sail on these and many others of the world's finest transatlantic liners. Despite my years of travel, however, the one voyage everyone wants to hear about is one that I don't even remember – the final voyage of the *Lusitania.* I boarded the liner on 1 May 1915 with my parents, siblings, and two nurses. Six days later, as a helpless three-month-old baby, I was scooped up and saved from death by a wonderfully brave woman, my nurse Alice Lines.

After the sinking, Alice and my father searched through the morgues in Queenstown looking for my two sisters and Alice's undernurse, Greta. They were never found. The shock of losing two children was a severe blow to my parents, but they persevered and led fulfilling lives. My nurse Alice and I remained firm friends for the next eighty-two years until her passing in 1997.

Having known the author for fifteen years, I was very pleased to be asked to write this foreword. Eric has done an outstanding job of researching and telling the story of this great liner. The photos presented here take me back to a day when travel was a more civilized experience. On this the ninetieth anniversary of the tragedy, this remarkable book pays tribute to the shipyard workers who created her; the crew who sailed her; and the men, women, and children who were lost. Congratulations, Eric, on a job well done.

Even with ninety years behind me, the sinking of the *Lusitania* stands as a pivotal moment in my life, one that changed my family forever. Despite all I have done and all I have seen, in the end, all points lead back to that long-ago day in May off the southern coast of Ireland.

The Honourable Mrs Audrey Pearl Lawson Johnston
Bedfordshire
May 2005

PREFACE

The name 'Lusitania' is synonymous with tragedy. Ninety years ago, her torpedoing stunned the civilized world, hitting home with a fury and taking over a thousand innocents to their deaths. The sinking was something from which the world never fully recovered.

Despite her significant place in maritime history, almost nothing has been written that concentrates on *Lusitania* as a living vessel and not as a target of war. Although this book gives an overview of the ship's history both before and after the sinking, the disaster and the political repercussions that followed fall outside the scope of this volume. The tragedy and its aftermath are, however, well covered in numerous other works.

Having researched *Lusitania* for the past twenty years, I found that full justice could not be done to the overwhelming magnitude of the story in a single volume. The sheer amount of information is too much for any publisher to reasonably put into print. Because of this, a companion web site to this volume has been developed to tell more of the story of this great ship and the people who sailed in her. Please visit www.northatlanticrun.com.

During the course of my research, I was very fortunate to locate twelve survivors of the sinking as well as dozens of relatives of both survivors and victims. It has been an amazing experience to learn about such a momentous event in history from the people who lived through it. On 7 May 1990, the 75th anniversary of the disaster, I met the last two first-class passengers – Alice Lines Drury and Audrey Pearl Lawson Johnston. Alice was an eighteen-year-old nurse for the Pearl family, and Audrey was the three-month-old baby she saved. Touching on the disaster only briefly during the first few hours of the visit, shortly after 2 p.m., we walked into the garden with Alice holding my arm. It was a beautifully clear day, and looking up into the sky, she casually remarked: 'It was a day just like today...'. Alice then related her experience of that terrible afternoon seventy-five years before to the minute that she stood on the deck of *Lusitania* as the liner sank beneath her.

Just over three years later, I found myself on a research vessel off the Old Head of Kinsale as historian for the two-week-long 1993 expedition. The opportunity of examining *Lusitania*'s remains first hand from a submersible has been given to only a lucky few, and I could not have imagined what an impact that experience would have on me. After two dives to the wreck, the liner and her story took on an entirely new, more personal dimension. Those events, more than anything else, changed the way I look at *Lusitania*.

Lusitania died a century ago. Yet through the photographs on these pages, we can, in some small way, transport ourselves back in time and imagine the pride felt by the Empire as Cunard's new leviathan conquered the Atlantic. It is with that in mind that this book was written.

Eric Sauder
Winterville, NC
May 2005

NOTES

For ease of reading and continuity, the present-day city of Cóbh (pronounced 'cove'), Ireland, is referred to throughout as Queenstown, the name of the city at the time of the disaster.

All of the opinions expressed herein are those of the author. Although every reasonable effort has been made to acknowledge copyright holders, errors can be made. The information contained in this book has been gathered from a large number of sources throughout the world and with the help of a great many people. Any source, even the memories of survivors of the sinking, is fallible. It is not the intent of the author for this work to be a definitive, comprehensive record of the history of *Lusitania*. Numerous events can be disputed, and alternative views are always welcome.

All quotes are copied verbatim from period sources. The spelling and punctuation of the original has been retained.

All images in this book are from the author's collection unless otherwise noted.

ACKNOWLEDGEMENTS

This book would have been impossible to write without help from dozens of people all over the world. My sincere thanks to the following: Audrey Pearl Lawson Johnston, *Lusitania* survivor and friend, for writing my foreword. Her generosity over the years has been unmatched, and our many visits are among my most treasured memories. Brian Hawley, whose enthusiasm made this book possible. Without his help and support, this work would not be what it is. Patrick O'Sullivan, whose incredible knowledge of *Lusitania* and her cargo has always been a precious resource and who has been one of the most generous supporters of my research through the years. Geoff Whitfield, whose encyclopedic database of the passengers and crew of *Lusitania* has proved invaluable in many difficult situations. Campbell McCutcheon for believing that another *Lusitania* book was needed. His patience throughout this project has been much appreciated. Brian Soye and Oliver Salzmann at Madison Press Books for allowing the use of Ken Marschall's amazing paintings.

Although most illustrations in the book come from my own collection, a few people generously lent photographs to fill in some gaps: Leigh Bishop (www.deepimage.co.uk), Robert Forrest, Gordon Ghareeb, Brian Hawley (www.luxurylinerrow.com), the late Walter Lord, Lars Froberg Mortensen, and Richard Woods.

Sincere thanks to those who have helped me over the years in ways too numerous to mention: George Behe, Julie Bowring, Margie Clark, Andrew Cockburn, Robert and Colleen Collier, Pat and Rose Ann Cook, Margaret Frankum, Phil Gowan, Ben Holme, Jemma Hyder, Jack Johnston, Dan Knowlton, Paul Latimer, Don Lynch, Cathy Offinger, Fr. Roberto Pirrone, Joyce Ramsbottom, Noel Ray, Kathy Savadel, Inger Sheil, Parks Stephenson, Maureen Watry, Jane Woods, and Richard Woods.

A heartfelt thanks to all the survivors of the sinking whom I have had the privilege of meeting and corresponding with: Chrissie Aitken Barnett, Desmond Cox, Alice Lines Drury, Avis Dolphin Foley, Elsie Hook Hadland, Frank Hook, Audrey Pearl Lawson Johnston, Barbara Anderson McDermott, Cecil Richards, Edythe Williams Wachtel, John Edward Williams, and Nancy Wickings-Smith Woods.

Finally to Mom and Dad without whose love and support none of this would have been possible.

ONE

BIRTH OF A
LEGEND

From the moment the paddle steamer *Britannia* left Liverpool on her first regularly scheduled transatlantic passenger voyage on 4 July 1840, the Cunard Steamship company dominated North Atlantic passenger travel. With almost no serious long-term challengers through the nineteenth century, travelers flocked to the company as a reliable and, more important, safe way to cross the Atlantic. In 1897, however, the British, who had long basked in their maritime superiority, were struck a serious blow. That year, a German shipyard produced the gleaming new four-funneled liner *Kaiser Wilhelm der Grosse*, which immediately became not only the largest liner on the Atlantic but also the fastest. For an island empire that depended on 'ruling the waves' for survival, Britain was placed in an unpleasant position. For the next decade, as the Germans built larger and finer ships, the situation became steadily worse. Britain, the greatest empire the world had ever known and which could count its age as several centuries, was not able to compete with the Germany of Kaiser Wilhelm II, a country not yet forty years old.

In 1902 another shock occurred. American financier J.P. Morgan began buying transatlantic shipping lines, including Cunard's chief British rival, the White Star Line, to form a huge international trust called the International Mercantile Marine (IMM). A few companies were able to remain independent of the conglomerate, but because of the huge pressures exerted by Morgan, those that did quickly came to agreements with the mighty Morgan Trust. For the time being, the only major transatlantic British line to remain free from the powerful hold of the IMM was Cunard. Something obviously had to be done before they, too, fell into American hands. Since the debut of the *Kaiser Wilhelm der Grosse* five years earlier, Britain had been put to shame repeatedly as German shipyards built liner after liner, each one larger, faster, and more impressive than the last. Seizing a golden opportunity and riding a growing wave of nationalism, Cunard's brilliant chairman, Lord Inverclyde, put his plan into action.

With Morgan's ambitions well known, Inverclyde approached the British government with a proposition. Under what became known as the Cunard Agreement, the government lent the shipping line £2,600,000 at 2¾ per cent for the construction of two mammoth new vessels, which would become *Lusitania* and *Mauretania*. The government also agreed to pay Cunard an annual subsidy of £150,000 to maintain both liners in war-readiness as well as an additional mail subsidy of £68,000 per year. Not willing to let Cunard have a free ride, however, the government came to the negotiating table with some stipulations to which the shipping line had to agree. First, and most importantly with the shadow of Morgan looming over them, Cunard had to remain a wholly owned British Company for the duration of the twenty-year agreement. The two new liners could be taken over by the Admiralty for war service at a moment's notice, and both vessels were to be constructed so they could be fitted with twelve 6in, quick-firing guns in time of war. The engine and boiler rooms of each liner as well as the rudder were to be placed below the waterline. In addition, coal bunkers were to be run along either side of both ships to absorb enemy gun fire. Aside from the engineers, all 'certificated' officers on the two new liners and 'not less than one half of the crew' were required to belong to the Royal Naval Reserve or the Royal Naval Fleet Reserve. Having little choice if they wanted to compete with the German lines, Cunard agreed. Once the entire agreement was hammered out and with the signed contract in hand, designing the liners began.

Built to compete directly with the German four stackers that had ruled the Atlantic for nearly a decade, in many ways, *Lusitania* revolutionized ocean travel. The most important of her firsts was that she was able to cross the Atlantic in under five days, and by the end of her second round-trip voyage, she had smashed every existing transatlantic record held by the Germans, leaving no doubt about who

In 1897, Germany entered the transatlantic speed race with the first four-stacker ever built, Norddeutscher Lloyd's *Kaiser Wilhelm der Grosse*, which easily eclipsed Cunard's *Campania* and *Lucania* in both size and speed. Upon entering service in 1900, Hapag's *Deutschland* wrested the Blue Riband from her Norddeutscher Lloyd rival, and like *Lusitania*, the record-breaking *Deutschland* was plagued with vibration problems.

controlled the Atlantic. Interior designers rather than shipyard committees created unheard of luxury in her first-class accommodation, and even third class, which had until then been called 'steerage,' far exceeded the conditions in which her poorest passengers had lived their entire lives. Included in these lower-class 'luxuries' were flush toilets, well-rounded meals, and real mattresses.

Originally conceived with three funnels and triple screws, various prototypes for *Lusitania* and *Mauretania* were proposed, but as the design progressed, one question always remained unanswered: What type of engines would drive the largest and, hopefully, fastest vessels the world had ever seen? The natural inclination was install something that had been tried and proved – the reciprocating engine. The problem was that liners had become so fast and so large that reciprocating engines had, for all intents and purposes, reached the upper limit of their size. The only other possible option to power the new record breakers was the newly invented steam turbine.

Premiered at the Spithead Naval Review in 1897, the turbine was still in its infancy, and although installed successfully in a few British naval vessels, it had been used in only one or two medium-sized passenger liners. As the size and complexity of the two new Cunarders grew, however, the company wasn't left with many options. Turbines seemed the only way to go. Still not willing to stake their reputation on a relatively untried propulsion system and because so much time and expense were being spent on these two new ships, whose failure to perform for any reason would be considered a serious blow to British pride, not to mention profits, Cunard's board of directors decided to experiment. Cunard had recently decided to build two sister ships of about 19,500 tons, *Caronia* and *Carmania*. Although nearly identical in every way, the ships were each fitted with a different type of propulsion plant. *Carmania* was equipped with three propellers and turbines, but *Caronia* received twin screws and quadruple-expansion reciprocating engines. After closely monitoring the coal consumption, average speeds, and performance of the two new ships through several months of service, it was found that *Carmania* consistently achieved nearly a full knot more than her sister at the same fuel consumption.

Not wanting to delay *Lusitania*'s delivery date, Cunard authorized the shipyard to begin construction of the liner while the data from *Carmania* and *Caronia* were being gathered and analyzed. Unlike most other ships, whose bows and sterns rose at approximately the same rate, work was concentrated on the forward end of *Lusitania*'s hull while construction of the stern lagged by several months in order to give the designers more time to hammer out the exact arrangement of her propulsion machinery, using *Carmania* as a guide post.

Thursday, 7 June 1906, dawned clear and warm with a light cooling breeze. It was perfect launch weather. The huge hull stood poised on the ways, and her hull number '367,' by which she was still officially known, was prominently displayed. Because of the importance of the event, John Brown & Co. had declared a holiday for its workers and issued each employee two passes for the launch. The gates to the yard opened at 11 a.m., and shortly afterwards every platform and space where a good view could be obtained had been taken. Postcard vendors slowly worked their way through the gathering crowd, selling images of the ship in various stages of construction to the tens of thousands of people who were on hand to witness the history-making event. Cameras were everywhere, and an elaborate apparatus was installed high above on one of the huge cranes to catch a bird's-eye view of the launch for reproduction on the 'fluttering films'. Located discreetly to the side, just in case, was the Clydebank Fire Brigade.

A few minutes before high tide, Mary, Lady Inverclyde, climbed to the launch platform, which was draped in crimson bunting, relieved by blue and gold trim. As the widow of Cunard's former chairman, she had agreed to christen the ship despite still being in mourning for her husband who had passed away about eight months before. At 12:30 p.m., she pressed an electric button, releasing a bottle against the starboard bow and sending the liner on her way in front of the 600 official guests of the launch party.

There was no perceptible movement at first, but the sound of creaking echoed across the river. Then from the crowd came a hushed whisper and the words 'she's moving.' Amid the ringing cheers of the spectators, the 16,000-ton hull gathered momentum, the stern dipping deeply into the water. There was a slight smoking of the ways near the water when the stern became buoyant. Her stem then left the ways, and she was afloat. Once she came to a stop, tugs

As early as January of 1902, mention was made during a meeting of Cunard's shipbuilding sub-committee of a proposal for two new liners for the Atlantic run, which would have 'increased protection' if employed as armed cruisers. By that October, serious discussions began about the 'two new fast steamers' to be built under an agreement with His Majesty's Government. They were to be triple screw and have three funnels with a speed of about 25 knots. The proposed dimensions were 750ft x 75ft although it was noted that the beam might have to be increased because of concerns about stability.

moved her a few hundred feet to the fitting out basin. While being interviewed by newspaper reporters shortly after the ceremony, a spokesman for John Brown proclaimed that, in the view of the builders, the launch was 'practically perfect.'

Immediately after the ship began her journey to the fitting out basin, 500 invited guests were ushered to a special luncheon which was served in the yard's moulding loft. The room was decorated with foliage and flowering plants, and the table decorations were composed of crimson and white roses, pale blue irises, lily of the valley, and maiden hair fern. At the banquet, Sir Charles MacLaren, deputy chairman of John Brown presided and proposed 'success to the *Lusitania* and prosperity to the Cunard Company.' In his reply, William Watson, who had succeeded Lord Inverclyde as chairman of Cunard, thanked John Brown for the splendid work they had done. He also made special mention of the gratitude they all had for the efforts of the late Lord Inverclyde without whose foresight and skill the ship would never have been built.

Elation ran high in the local pubs that day. One newspaper pointed out that the 'Clydebank public houses were well patronized' and that 'many a pint was no doubt raised to the new Cunard queen.'

Cunard's chairman, Lord Inverclyde, was the driving force behind the construction of *Lusitania* and *Mauretania*. Unfortunately, he never saw his dream become reality. He died on 8 October 1905, eight months before *Lusitania*'s launch. Through his outstanding business acumen, he set the stage for Cunard's greatest successes for the next six decades.

In mid-December 1902, the first tenders were received by Cunard from four shipbuilding yards that were being considered to construct the new Cunard steamers. They were Messrs Vickers Sons & Maxim Ltd; Messrs John Brown & Co. Ltd; The Fairfield Shipbuilding & Engineering Co. Ltd; and Messrs C.S. Swan & Hunter Ltd, Wallsend. In the end, the contracts were awarded to John Brown and Swan Hunter. The keel of *Lusitania*, which had been laid down by Lord Inverclyde, sits in the foreground on the slipway. From this metal 'spine,' the great vessel grew. In the background, work is rapidly progressing on the new Cunarder *Carmania*.

Cunard's general superintendent frequently shuttled between Liverpool, Clydebank, and the Tyne to ensure that construction of the two liners progressed on schedule. By mid-January, 1907, Mr Duncan, who had been chosen as chief engineer of *Lusitania*, had come ashore and moved to Clydebank to oversee construction of her power train. Cunard received weekly progress reports from him as well as the Lloyd's surveyor who had been assigned to the vessel.

As a reserve naval vessel, *Lusitania* had to be as responsive as possible to bridge orders. In a design feature frequently used by the Royal Navy, Cunard's naval architect removed the part of the liner's keel called the 'deadwood,' thereby forming an arch just forward of the rudder. This permitted tighter turning circles and made the ship more maneuverable.

Throughout construction of the liner, a few delays were caused by work stoppages, the longest of which was a seven-week strike by the boiler makers and iron workers that began on 1 October 1906. During the strike, their duties were carried out 'to complete satisfaction' by the senior apprentices. By 22 November, it was reported that the ironworkers had returned to work.

At the beginning of May, 1906, the propeller shafts and rudder were shipped into place, and just a week before the scheduled launch date, Cunard's general superintendent reported that he had 'examined the work in progress on [*Lusitania*] on the 28th instant at Clydebank; that the rudder is hung, propeller blades in place and all completed for launching; and that the sliding ways are in place, and the vessel ready for putting in the water any time there is a suitable tide.'

An unusual view of *Lusitania's* propellers just before launch. A few specially invited and well-dressed guests are allowed a close-up examination of the hull. Despite the dirty conditions of the shipyard, this was an era when men and women still wore their best while on an outing.

The names *Lusitania* and *Mauretania* were decided upon on 15 February 1906, but it was not until 23 May of that year that the confusion over how *Mauretania* should be spelled was finally resolved.

The question of the spelling of the name of the New Fast Steamer now being built by Messrs Swan Hunter & Co. was considered, and it appearing that the opinion of authorities is that the name should be spelled 'Mauretania,' not 'Mauritania' as previously decided, it was decided that the name should be with an 'e,' i.e. 'Mauretania.'

For several hours before the launch, workmen swarmed around the ship, knocking out the keel blocks, shores, and bilge blocks, which supported the liner during construction.

With the Union Jack fluttering in the breeze and band playing *Rule Britannia*, Lady Inverclyde broke a bottle of wine on the starboard bow and christened the liner 'Lusitania', a name taken from the ancient Roman province that occupied modern-day Portugal. A few moments later, a slight creaking was heard, and the great hull began its journey.

The launch of *Lusitania* was described by one newspaper as 'an event of…national importance.' Britain's maritime pride, having been seriously wounded by the Germans, was restored, and the Empire remained supreme on the Atlantic for the next twenty-two years.

TWO

AN ENORMOUS
GAMBLE

Four years of planning, preparation, and construction were over in less than three minutes. To the immense relief of everyone at Cunard and John Brown's yard, the launch was a success in every respect. Once clear of the ways and brought to a stop by immense drag chains that had been used to launch Brunel's *Great Eastern* nearly fifty years before, *Lusitania* was maneuvered into the fitting-out basin by a bevy of tugs where she would rest for the next year while hundreds of workmen swarmed aboard each day to ensure that the pride of Britain's merchant fleet would be completed on time. Delays could be costly, not only in prestige but also in profits. Stiff daily penalties would be assessed on the builders if the ship were not finished according to schedule. Because of tidal conditions, *Lusitania* had to depart John Brown's yard before she was finished. She left for the first time at the beginning of June 1907, and after a successful journey down the Clyde, the liner anchored at the Tail o' the Bank at Gourock where most of the remaining work was carried out.

Lusitania then underwent two sets of trials, one 'secret' and one public. Having just designed and built not only the largest but also the most technologically advanced ship of the day, Cunard and the builders agreed to hold a series of secret trials away from the prying eyes of the public and press in case the liner did not perform as expected. A mechanical failure or breakdown would have been catastrophic for public relations. Once any kinks were worked out, a second set of 'official' trials would be held. Uppermost in the minds of the government representatives was the fact that, having lent so much money to Cunard for the construction of *Lusitania* and *Mauretania*, Parliament and the Admiralty wanted to make sure that she performed up to the contract specifications and that there would be no alteration of any of the trial data in favor of the builders.

After testing her anchors for the Board of Trade at the Tail o' the Bank, she made a number of 'secret' test trips over the measured mile at Skelmorlie. After these successful runs, *Lusitania* embarked her first passengers for a 740-mile jaunt around Ireland. Upon completion of this two-day trip, her passengers disembarked via the Cunard tender *Skirmisher* in Liverpool. *Lusitania* then departed for her official trials on 29 July. So much was riding on the success of the new liner that these speed tests were longer and more comprehensive than usual, lasting 48 hours at full speed.

Her first set of trials consisted of four 303-mile runs between Corsewall Lighthouse, near Loch Ryan, and Longship Lighthouse at Land's End in Cornwall. Beginning at nearly midnight on Monday, *Lusitania* steamed southward and reached Land's End before noon on Tuesday, averaging 26.4 knots for the course. She then turned around and reached Scotland soon after midnight on Tuesday in a half gale. Her average speed for her first northbound trip was 24.3 knots. On her second run southward, the time from the first run differed only by two minutes and a tenth of a knot, averaging 26.3. On the return northward, a fresh headwind had picked up but she still performed better than on her first run north, achieving an average of 24.6 knots. Her average speed over the entire 1,200 mile course was 25.4 knots under the same conditions and load as would be experienced on the Atlantic.

On 1 August, *Lusitania* began her second speed trials and made two runs in each direction between the Corsewall Light and the Chicken Rock Light on the Isle of Man. On her first run, with a little help from the current, she achieved an astounding speed of 26.7 knots. On the return trip, the opposing tide made a slight difference, and her speed was 26.2 knots. The mean speed of 26.45 knots for the four runs was, in the words of one newspaper, 'a magnificent achievement'. She then did six quick jaunts between Holy Isle on the coast of Arran and Ailsa Craig, fully performing up to Cunard's, and more importantly the Admiralty's, requirements.

Since her trials began, *Lusitania* had steamed more than 2,000 miles and attained speeds of well over 25 knots. It was now clear to everyone involved that the huge gamble the liner represented would pay off handsomely and the ship would easily exceed her contract required speed of 24.5 knots.

Lusitania went into the Canada Dry Dock in Liverpool on 3 August for some maintenance and then returned to the Clyde to steam the mile at Skelmorlie once again. She then returned to Liverpool and anchored in the Sloyne, waiting patiently to show her paces. Because of the huge public demand to visit the liner, Cunard arranged a public viewing of the ship, which took place on 3 September, and the proceeds of ½ crown per person were given to various charities. Several large tenders were engaged from 11 a.m. to 4 p.m. to convey the crowds of curious Liverpudlians. The day was an immense success with visitors numbering about 10,000, which one local newspaper described as 'mainly a superior class of people.'

Four days later, the eyes of the world were on her as she sailed for New York and, hopefully, the record books.

The exact timing of the launch differs from source to source, but most agree that from the moment the bottle of wine was broken against *Lusitania*'s starboard bow until the huge 1,000-ton drag chains stopped her movement, a mere two minutes and forty-two seconds had passed. She entered the water at an average speed of 12.2ft per second.

Lusitania completely fills the length of the fitting-out basin at John Brown. Construction of the forward end of the superstructure is well advanced. All four funnels and the foremast were in place by 28 November 1906, but the main mast could not be shipped until the turbines were on board.

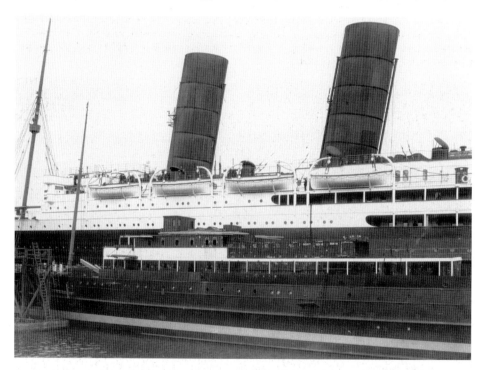

Judging from the surviving evidence, it seems that there were more construction problems with *Mauretania* than her sister. Swan Hunter was constantly asking for additional input from Cunard, and in March, 1906, Cunard's surveyor made a report to the directors that stated 'the work on this ship [*Mauretania*] is satisfactory but not so far advanced as in the *Lusitania*.'

From these two photos taken several months apart, one gets a superb view of the same area of the liner during different phases of construction. In the image above, work is proceeding on the second-class deck house, and construction has just begun on the first-class Smoking Room and Verandah Café. In the lower photo, the liner is nearly complete.

This photo, taken late during the ship's fitting out, shows *Lusitania* nearly complete, but the Verandah Café is still under construction. It was finally decided in February, 1907, to enclose the sides of the café and not leave it open to the elements.

Great interest was taken in *Lusitania*'s departure from the builder's yard and her journey to the Tail o' the Bank. For the previous twelve months, the Clyde Navigation Trust had been busy dredging the entire upper portion of the river to a uniform depth of 34ft at high water. Still, no little anxiety was felt in certain quarters because of concerns that the narrow channel might not be sufficiently deep and the ship might run aground. On her passage down the Clyde, the huge liner drew 29½ft.

Lusitania cleared the dock at John Brown at 11:50 a.m. and reached Greenock just under two hours later. Steaming down the Clyde at a rate of from 5 to 10 knots, Lusitania was accompanied by six tugs in case of mishap. Elaborate arrangements had been made for her departure, and everything passed without incident.

Crowds of curious locals lined the banks of the Clyde to watch Lusitania's progress down the river. The note on the back of this photo reads: 'These are not my taking, but there [sic] good photos nonetheless!! I've not had mine developed yet.'

Right: In this view, taken from the crow's nest while *Lusitania* was anchored at the Tail o' the Bank, the original configuration of the boats and ventilators can be seen. The skylight to the Officers' Smoke Room is in the foreground, and each of the dark mushroom vents around the perimeter of the bridge roof ventilated a different officer's cabin.

Below: In the event of it not being demonstrated during actual service during the first twelve months after delivery, that the ship is capable, on a draught not exceeding 33 feet 2½ inches, of maintaining a minimum average ocean speed of at least 24¾ knots per hour in moderate weather, the Builders shall pay to the Cunard Company as liquidated damages the following sums…

The penalties that could be assessed on John Brown for *Lusitania* not reaching her contract speeds were severe – £10,000 for every 1/10th of a knot under 24½ with a maximum fine of £100,000. *Lusitania's* trials took her on a course of over 2,000 miles during which she reached a top speed of 26.7 knots, more than two knots higher than her contract requirement of 24.5 knots.

Opposite

Top left: During an interview with the Director of Naval Construction for the Admiralty, Cunard's representative suggested that the ordinary pulley-and-chain-type telegraphs be employed on *Lusitania* and *Mauretania* as they were on the rest of the Cunard fleet. The Director, however, was adamant that the more-reliable Admiralty-pattern telegraph, which was worked by rods and miter wheels, should be the method adopted for the engine telegraphs because of their reliability and *Lusitania's* possible use as an armed cruiser. Under the conditions of the Government loan, Cunard had little choice. They relented and adopted the Admiralty's requirement. The difference in cost is what concerned Cunard. To supply *Lusitania* with ordinary engine telegraphs would have cost only £250. To outfit the ship with the type of telegraph required by the Admiralty, the cost was £2,000.

Top right: Lusitania's starting platform. It took a staff of over 300 to keep all the machinery on board in operation around the clock. The first high-pressure turbine was tested at the beginning of November, 1906, and was run at 204 revolutions per minute. The engineers reported that everything was satisfactory. By the middle of March, 1907, all the engine machinery was on board. The turbines on *Lusitania* consisted of over 990,000 hand-set blades. If these blades and their spacing pieces were laid end to end, they would reach 182 miles. The weight of the blades alone was over 97 tons, or about 194,000 pounds. To comply with Admiralty regulations, the main propelling and auxiliary machinery were located in nine separate watertight compartments.

Left: After the torpedo struck, it was in this area that Senior Second Engineer Andrew Cockburn found Chief Engineer Bryce. To quote from the British Inquiry:

Sir Edward Carson: What did you find there?
Andrew Cockburn: I found the Chief Engineer.
Carson: Was the place in darkness?
Cockburn: Yes, the place was in darkness.
Lord Mersey: The lights were out?
Cockburn: Yes, the lights were out, my Lord.
Carson: Where were you standing at that time?
Cockburn: Down the first grating in the engine room – down the first ladder.
Carson: Had you a conversation with the Chief Engineer?
Cockburn: Yes; he asked me what we could possibly do now.
Carson: And what did you say?
Cockburn: I said 'absolutely nothing.'

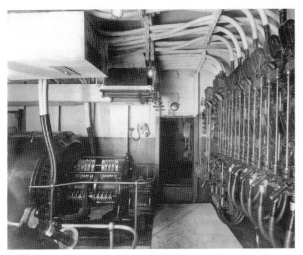

Left: Lusitania was outfitted with four 375kW turbo-generators, which were located on Orlop Deck aft. The turbo-generator room was divided in half by a watertight bulkhead in case of accident so that there was little chance of a total loss of power. Note the telephone on the far bulkhead. The bell above the watertight door rang to alert the engineer on duty that he was wanted on the phone.

Although clearly staged, this photo of a boiler room on board *Aquitania* gives a good idea of the harsh working conditions endured by members of the 'black gang'. The noise, heat, and filth are almost unimaginable today. *Lusitania* had four boiler rooms that contained twenty-five water-tube boilers – each of which was 17½ft in diameter. The boilers consumed coal at a rate of about 1,000 tons per day. As they were built, but before being placed on board, each one was tested to twice its working pressure of 195 pounds per square inch, and it was reported that they 'proved quite satisfactory'.

Lusitania and her sister *Mauretania* were similar in basic dimensions and arrangement. Each shipyard, however, was given a free hand to design their ship as long as the basic Admiralty requirements were met. Externally, the most obvious differences between the two vessels are the ventilators and the shape of the bridge front. The interior of each liner, however, had a very distinct personality. *Lusitania*'s architect, James Miller, chose plaster and gilding to create light, airy public rooms. Harold Peto, who designed *Mauretania*, had a very different philosophy. Through the use of dark woods and heavily carved moulding, Peto's interiors resembled a London gentlemen's club.

Above: After the phenomenal success of *Lusitania* and *Mauretania*, Cunard decided to forego building another record breaker and concentrate on luxury to compete head on with the White Star and Hamburg Amerika giants. The result was *Aquitania*, considered by many historians to be one of the finest liners ever built. Introduced in 1914, she was the only large transatlantic liner to serve in both world wars, finally being scrapped in 1950. (Photo by Everett Viez, courtesy of Gordon Ghareeb)

Right: It was during the pre-maiden voyage dry-docking in Liverpool that the white stripe just under her forecastle was painted black in order to bring her in line with the other ships of the fleet.

In this very early photo, *Lusitania* is docked in Liverpool. None of the alterations to her second-class superstructure have been made, and the white stripe under her forecastle has not yet been painted black. Note the bumper guard marked 'Cunard', which protected the starboard forward propeller from accidental damage.

A magnificent view showing the fine lines of *Lusitania*'s bow. It was in the area just forward of the tender that the torpedo fired from the U-20 struck. (Walter Lord Collection)

In this unusual image, one of double shell doors to the first-class entrance on E Deck can be seen. The closed door in the middle of the photo led into one of the firemen's entrances. Note the high-profile rivets used on the upper part of the hull. (Walter Lord Collection)

THREE

A Transatlantic
Debutante

The maiden departure of *Lusitania* was met everywhere with unanimous enthusiasm. Everywhere, that is, except the German Empire. Since the advent of the *Kaiser Wilhelm der Grosse* in 1897, Germany had ruled the Atlantic, and their first four-stacker had quickly put Britain's greatest ships, *Lucania* and *Campania*, to shame. For the next decade, the British Empire had to play 'second fiddle' to Germany. With the advent of *Lusitania*, it was now Britain's opportunity to turn the table.

At 9:10 pm., on 7 September 1907, under the command of Captain James B. Watt, *Lusitania* departed from the Prince's Landing Stage in Liverpool. Fully 200,000 people lined the shore and watched her steam down the Mersey, slowly picking up speed for her overnight journey to Queenstown, Ireland. After a brief call there to embark additional passengers and mail, *Lusitania* made her way out into the Atlantic, leaving some 200 travelers behind in Queenstown. They had arrived in the Irish port hoping to book last-minute passages, but all were disappointed. Everything on the voyage proceeded as expected, and during the following few days, *Lusitania* sighted and overtook a number of other liners heading for New York, including *Lucania*, *Amerika* and *La Provence*. On the morning of the eleventh, she also passed White Star's *Celtic*, which had sailed from Liverpool a full two days before *Lusitania*. After only three-and-a-half days of steaming, She had completely wiped out *Celtic*'s two-day head start.

For most of the crossing, the weather remained clear and calm, and each day Captain Watt slowly notched up the liner's speed. Anticipation of a record crossing was palpable on the great liner as she steadily neared the shores of North America. Then, a mere one day from her destination, all hopes for a record crossing were dashed. A heavy fogbank off Newfoundland forced Captain Watt to reduce speed. By the time *Lusitania* reached New York, she had made the crossing in five days and fifty-four minutes at an average speed of 23.01 knots, missing the *Deutschland*'s record by a mere thirty minutes.

The liner arrived at Sandy Hook at 8:50 a.m. on Friday, 13 September. Earlier, Cunard officials had cabled Captain Watt not to attempt to enter the Ambrose channel before dawn because she was the first inbound ship to use the newly dredged channel and there was a concern about the possibility of grounding. As she made her way through New York Harbor, it seemed as though everything that could float had come out to greet her. As *Lusitania* sailed past the Statue of Liberty, sirens sounded, guns were fired, and flags were unfurled. From the tower of the Singer Building, then the tallest structure in the world, an enormous flag was broken out, bearing the single word 'welcome.' Estimates were that 200 vessels escorted *Lusitania* to her berth, and during her passage through the harbor, her blue ensign was lowered continually in acknowledgement of the salutes. New York had never seen such a welcome.

Slowly steaming up the Hudson River, *Lusitania* reached Cunard's Pier 54 but continued up river past the pier. She then turned around, and using the force of the ebbing tide, Captain Watt slowly swung the liner into her berth. She finally docked at noon amid scenes of 'immense enthusiasm.'

Undoubtedly disappointed that *Lusitania* didn't take the Blue Riband, a Cunard spokesman dismissed reporters' questions and said that 'the performance of the *Lusitania* was eminently satisfactory for a first trip.' Cunard, he continued, did not intend for her to be pushed but preferred that the engineers should have an extended acquaintance with the ship before attempting to force high speeds.

On her return voyage to England, she again failed to take the coveted prize, but on her second crossing from Liverpool, the weather held, and *Lusitania* proved her paces by smashing every transatlantic record held by Germany and bringing the Blue Riband back to Great Britain. There was a triumphal demonstration in the first-class dining room on the final night of the record-breaking voyage. The passenger who presided over the historic event stated that 'although we applaud the *Deutschland* as the pacemaker, yet we cheer the *Lusitania* for beating her in this heroic struggle to wrest from the German giant the Blue Riband of the Atlantic. The lion is again master of the ocean highway and this English victory is one in which the whole world joins us.'

With great modesty, *Lusitania's* Purser Lancaster offered the following limerick as his personal contribution to the evening's festivities:

> There was a young man in Westphalia,
> Who had charge of much costly regalia,
> To his sweetheart he said,
> 'My dear, when we're wed,
> We'll call our first girl Lucy Tania.

On this voyage, *Lusitania* became the first ship in history to cross the Atlantic in under five days. According to a statement issued by Cunard, her average speed was 24.002 knots, and once *Mauretania* entered service that November, a friendly rivalry cropped up between the two sisters. *Lusitania* would set up a Blue Riband record only to lose it to *Mauretania* a short time later. For two years, they fought it out. In the end, however, it appeared to the public that the British-built

Surrounded by tugs, *Lusitania* warps into her berth at the completion of her maiden voyage. According to Cunard's official statement, 'the passage occupied 4d 19h 52m, and the average speed was 24.002 knots'. Shortly after the liner's arrival, Vernon Brown, American agent for Cunard, was interviewed and declared that *Lusitania* had made a wonderful trip but, he whispered, that 'she's got something up her sleeve yet.'

The day before *Lusitania* arrived in New York at the end of her maiden voyage, a number of newspapers ran a story about the Belfast shipyard of Harland & Wolff having signed a contract with the White Star Line to construct two new passenger liners for the Southampton-New York service. These vessels became *Olympic* and *Titanic*. *Olympic* is seen here at the end of her career, flying both the White Star and Cunard house flags. (Photo courtesy of Brian Hawley)

According to one newspaper correspondent, the Germans were quite insistent in reminding the public that two of their ships, the *Deutschland* and the *Kaiser Wilhelm II*, had each logged more miles on four consecutive days than *Lusitania* had on her maiden voyage. They also pointed out that the daily average speed of their two liners had not been beaten by the Cunarder.

Mauretania proved to be a fraction of a knot faster than her Scottish-built sister, but perhaps one of *Mauretania*'s masters, Captain S.G.S. McNeil, should have the final say:

In 1905 I was promoted to Chief Officer of the *Umbria*; and, after the *Lusitania* had made three voyages, I went as Chief Officer of her, a position I held from 1907 until I got command in the spring of 1911. I shall have much to say later on about the *Mauretania*; but I will state here that she was not a bit faster than the *Lusitania*. I made fifty-three voyages in the *Lusitania* as Chief Officer; and was subsequently nearly five years in the *Mauretania* as Staff-Captain and Captain. Passengers frequently told me that they always understood that the *Mauretania* was the faster. This wrong impression was probably brought about by the fact that the *Lusitania*, on her first

An exquisite close-up view of *Lusitania*'s stern just after her maiden voyage. Over 5,000 people daily flocked to visit the liner, including Mark Twain, who was a guest of Cunard. Twain showed a great interest in everything he saw, and when the tour was finished, he drew a long breath and said: 'I guess I'll have to tell Noah about it when I see him.'

For days curious New Yorkers came to look at the greatest ship in the world. Some American passengers were loud in singing the praises of the new Cunarder. To them, her comfort, speed, and steadiness were unsurpassed. One maiden voyage passenger, who had crossed the Atlantic ninety times, was heard to remark: 'The Cunard Company has now got the Germans skinned to the teeth.'

eight voyages, did not have the type of propeller blade that the *Mauretania* had. When the new ones were shipped the former's averages improved considerably, and I remember three of them were 25.89 knots with only a decimal difference.

Following her maiden voyage, *Lusitania* settled into a comfortable routine and instantly became a favorite with the traveling public. Her light, airy interiors, her punctuality, and her reliability made her one of the most popular vessels on the Atlantic despite the introduction of larger liners. Less than eight years after she entered service, however, the actions of a single man would change her name from one that maritime nations envied to a rallying cry in the fight against the 'barbarism of the blood-stained huns.'

Standing on precarious wooden platforms rigged from above, workers begin coaling *Mauretania* while docked in New York. Each load of coal, amounting to thousands of tons per voyage, was lifted and put on board by hand.

Funnels, funnels everywhere… On 14 October 1909, *Lusitania* and *Mauretania* both made an appearance in Liverpool and were berthed together for a brief time. It was one of the rare instances the two sisters were together.

Opposite: After arriving in New York, several passengers complained to the press about the heat of many of the staterooms on board although it was not specified if this was throughout the voyage or just before arrival. When *Lusitania* reached New York, the temperature was around 85 degrees. One newspaper reporter who had been on board for the crossing complained about distressing vibration when the vessel was going full speed. He noted that 'one can scarcely write in the saloon. There are, however, some parts of the ship that are not affected.'

A beautiful view of *Lusitania*'s Boat Deck as seen from the port bridge wing. The liner had recently docked in Liverpool and is discharging her passengers. This is an early view as evidenced by lifeboat No.16 being in the foreground. As constructed, *Lusitania*'s lifeboats were numbered in reverse order from other ships at the time – the high numbered boats were forward and the lower numbers aft.

After arriving in Liverpool and discharging her passengers at the landing stage, *Lusitania* made her way to one of two buoys in the Sloyne – Cunard A or Cunard B. Once there, a bow anchor was removed, and the loose end of the chain was attached to the buoy securing the vessel.

First Class

Following the convention of the day, *Lusitania* was divided into three classes – first, second, and third. First class was located amidships and occupied the largest portion of the vessel. With a number of large well-appointed public rooms to choose from, it was estimated that first-class passengers on board *Lusitania* had fifty per cent more living space than on any previous liner.

To ensure that their premier liners would be the finest afloat, steamship companies often spied on the competition. This was a fairly common practice at the time, and representatives from the various shipping lines frequently visited or sailed on their competitors' ships to get new ideas to outdo their rivals. For example, Leonard Peskett, Cunard's senior naval architect, visited White Star's *Olympic* on several occasions while designing *Aquitania*. Thomas Andrews, of Harland & Wolff, who later lost his life in the *Titanic* disaster, sailed to New York on *Lusitania* and took copious notes, including such minute technical details as the distance the expansion joints flexed in various types of weather.

In November 1907, a twenty-one-year-old William Francis Gibbs, who designed the record-breaker, s.s. *United States* over four decades later, sailed to Liverpool on *Lusitania*, and returned to New York on *Mauretania*, taking notes the entire way. His young mind was already looking forward to the day when a ship of his making would sweep the seas and bring the Blue Riband back to the United States.

Even upper management took part. In late 1904, Alfred Booth, a Cunard director and later chairman of the company, sailed to the United States and back on board the White Star liner *Baltic* specifically to obtain ideas to incorporate into Cunard's two new express liners. Upon his return, he made a number of suggestions for the interior design and layout of *Lusitania*. Because Booth was so well known in shipping circles and no doubt received the best possible service on board *Baltic*, he then secretly sent Cunard's general superintendent to New York on the *Kaiser Wilhelm II* and had him return on White Star's *Cedric*. The superintendent's anonymity allowed Cunard to obtain a more realistic impression of the service on board their competitors.

The following interior photographs are presented to give the reader a chance to see Cunard's vision of the perfect liner. *Lusitania*'s interiors represented the culmination of over sixty years of passenger experience on the Atlantic, and although larger ships were built, she remained a firm favorite until her loss.

Port Regal Suite

The finest accommodations on board were the two Regal Suites on Promenade Deck. At the end of May, 1906, James Miller, *Lusitania*'s interior designer, attended a meeting of Cunard's shipbuilding committee and presented his designs for the first-class Lounge, Regal Suites, and *en suite* rooms. They were approved by the directors subject to certain modifications, which were duly made. One interesting note to survive from the meeting is that 'it was directed that the "Jalousies" in Staterooms and Bathrooms be arranged so as to prevent any "spying" '. Consisting of two bedrooms, a sitting room, a dining room, private bath, lavatory, and a pantry, each Regal Suite was decorated in various popular period styles. Hardwood paneling, original art, charming Wedgwood cameos, and touches of gilding made these rooms unequaled to anything at sea.

B-48. Final voyage occupants:
Albert and Gladys Bilicke.

B-52. Final voyage occupants:
Charles and Frances Fowles.

B-54. Final voyage occupants:
Caroline Hickson Kennedy and
her sister Miss Hickson.

The contracts to outfit the suites and special staterooms were awarded to three different companies – Trollope & Sons, Waring & Gillow, and Wylie & Lochhead. The cost estimates submitted varied by a wide margin. Waring & Gillow's quote was £8,458 8s od for eighteen rooms, but Trollope's cost was £10,535 5s 1d for the same number of cabins. In contrast, Wylie & Lochhead asked £5,841 15s od for their sixteen staterooms. Cunard management considered Trollope's estimates much too high and requested that they requote at a lower price. Although resisting at first, Trollope eventually reduced their total contract price to £8,922. John Brown outfitted the ten remaining special cabins on Promenade Deck at a cost of about £4,000. The construction total for the sixty-two special rooms on *Lusitania*'s Promenade Deck was £28,835 8s 1d, including miscellaneous expenses, compared to those on *Mauretania*, which cost about £26,000.

Right: B-47. Final voyage occupant: Lady Marguerite Allan. Lady Allan's two daughters, Gwen and Anna, were in the connecting cabin, B-49, which can be seen through the door.

Below left: B-51. Final voyage occupants: Dr Frederick and Mabel Pearson.

Below right: B-53. Final voyage occupants: James and Georgina Young.

En-Suite Rooms

Located just aft of the Regal Suites on Promenade Deck were *Lusitania's en suite* rooms. Aside from the Regal Suites, they were the finest cabins on board and included such 'luxuries' as running water, telephones, attached bathrooms, and lavatories.

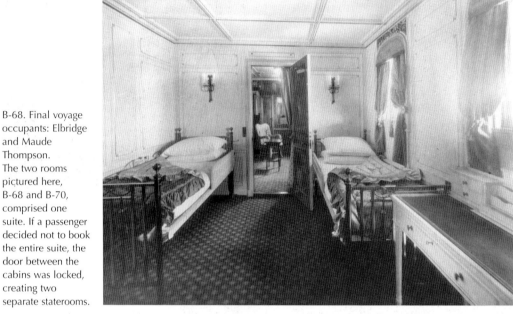

B-68. Final voyage occupants: Elbridge and Maude Thompson.
The two rooms pictured here, B-68 and B-70, comprised one suite. If a passenger decided not to book the entire suite, the door between the cabins was locked, creating two separate staterooms.

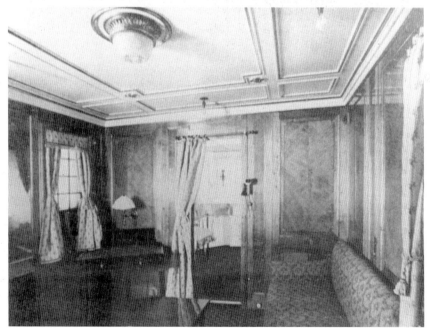

B-70. Final voyage occupants: Elbert and Alice Hubbard.

Above left: B-67. Final voyage occupant: Alfred Gwynne Vanderbilt. He booked the entire *en suite* room, which included B-65, B-67, and the adjoining bathroom and toilet.

Above right: B-77. Final voyage occupants: Stuart and Leslie Mason. Through the connecting door, Charles Frohman's cabin can be seen.

Left: Located just forward of the Dining Room, cabin D-36 on Upper Deck was typical of the first-class staterooms on board. If the upper berth was not needed, it could be folded up and out of the way to give a feeling of more space in the cabin. This was one of the very few rooms to have a telephone and a separate area for the wash basin. In fact, telephones were placed only in the suites and a few of the better staterooms, and to install just these few phones cost £1,026. To have put them into all first-class cabins would have cost £2,025.

Located on Boat Deck, cabin A-16 was occupied by William and Sara Hodges on *Lusitania*'s last crossing. Their two young sons, William and Dean, were in the connecting cabin. The entire family was lost in the disaster. In the photo below, the remains of the sink from this cabin can be seen on the wreck today. The area of Boat Deck on which this cabin sat has shifted and is now some ninety degrees out of alignment with the rest of the hull. (Wreck photo by Leigh Bishop)

Located on Boat Deck between the third and fourth funnels was *Lusitania*'s Lounge and Music Room, which was the main hub of activity for first class. It was decorated in a Georgian style with veneered mahogany walls, and to offset the dark wood paneling, soothing tones of soft greens and yellows were chosen for upholstery and carpeting. Massive marble fireplaces stood at the ends of the room, and centered over each were beautiful enamels by Alexander Fisher. The subjects of these panels were 'The Glory of the Sunrise' and 'The Conquest of the Sea.' The total cost for the two enamels was £275, including the silver frames.

A twenty-foot-high barrel vault surmounted the room and was decorated with delicate plasterwork of water pixies, shells, and fruits of the sea. The dome was divided into twelve stained-glass panels, each representing a month of the year.

Left: Long vistas were used wherever possible on *Lusitania* to help give a feeling of spaciousness. A passenger could stand at the aft end of the Smoking Room and look through several public rooms all the way to the forward end of Boat Deck.

Below: An unusually rare photograph of the aft starboard bay in *Lusitania*'s first-class Lounge, published here for the first time since 1907. The four semi-circular bays were each outfitted as separate sitting areas with groups of easy chairs, sofas, and tables. Notice the rods to keep the furniture in place during rough weather.

Because of the large number of first-class passengers to be carried on board *Lusitania*, it was necessary to arrange the Dining Saloon on two levels, Shelter Deck and Upper Deck. Decorated in the style of Louis XVI, the room was relatively small compared to later liners, but Miller achieved a remarkable feeling of spaciousness through his use of white enameled walls, gilding, mirrors, and an enormous dome overhead.

At a meeting of the Cunard directors held in Clydebank two days after the launch, it was decided that the gilding in the Dining Saloon was 'to be executed by French Gilders and the gold to be toned down to the old French color. The carving and ornamental mouldings to be carved from the solid and not to be of [plaster].' Despite the additional expense of £1,800 for the hand-carved decoration, Cunard spent the extra money because of the much greater maintenance cost for plaster over time. The only places decorative plaster was used was in the domes and the parts of the ship 'where there will be no likelihood of it having to be removed for access to electrical wiring or probability of leakage...'.

Located on Shelter Deck just forward of the first-class Entrance was a children's nursery, which doubled as the servants' dining room and could accommodate forty people at a sitting. Its decoration was also Louis XVI although of a much simpler design.

In the preliminary design, the upper level of the Dining Saloon was intended to be an exclusive à la carte restaurant. At some point, however, this idea was abandoned, and although not advertised as such, the upper level became, in the minds of the traveling public, a more exclusive part of the room.

Electric lights were fitted behind the sliding glass screens in front of the portholes to simulate daylight even at night, and because of the heat in New York during the summer, electric 'punkahs,' or fans, were considered and even approved by Cunard. The wiring was run during construction, but the fans were not installed until after the ship was in service.

This photo was taken while docked in New York on one of her early voyages, and one of the most interesting things is the pattern of china on the tables. Surprisingly, it is not the blue and pink floral pattern that some researchers have claimed was created for her maiden voyage, but rather the commonly seen blue-delft style used on earlier Cunarders.

An extraordinary view of the dome in *Lusitania*'s first-class Dining Saloon. Rising 30ft above the center of the room, the dome was beautifully embellished with fine plaster details and four paintings in the style of François Boucher that represented the four seasons. Where possible, the use of plaster rather than carved wood not only reduced weight but construction costs as well.

As originally conceived, *Lusitania* had no mirrors in her first-class Dining Saloon. Because of the 'great width of the ship, and the inability to obtain overhead light, [that] will make the saloons somewhat dark…,' lighting was of primary importance. To solve this problem, Miller recommended that mirrors be installed in strategic points around the room. This was approved on 21 November 1906. He also suggested that paintings be placed on the outboard sides of the ventilator shafts, but this idea was ultimately rejected, probably as a cost-saving measure. A light fixture identical to the sconces seen in this photo was recovered from the wreck in 1982.

Situated forward of the first-class entrance on Boat Deck, the Writing Room and Library of *Lusitania* was, in the opinion of many designers of the time, among the most pleasing rooms on board. Above the rose carpet, inset panels of grey silk covered the walls, and beautifully etched decorative glass panels hid the outside windows.

Following the custom of the day, first-class passengers were expected to send a card or letter to relatives back home before sailing, inlaid mahogany writing desks being provided for this time-honored ritual. Ample amounts of writing paper and envelopes were supplied free of charge, and postcards of the ship were available and could be purchased from the library steward. In addition to being a quiet spot to write letters, this room also served as the ship's library with a well-stocked bookcase on the aft wall. Books could be checked out for the voyage, but passengers were 'earnestly requested' to return them promptly because the steward was charged for any that went missing.

First-Class Staircase

Elegantly decorated in black, white and gold and offset with rose upholstery, the first-class entrance on Boat Deck was supplied with wicker chairs, tables, and potted palms, giving this area the feeling of an outdoor verandah. Oil paintings were to be fitted on either side of the fireplace, but as a cost-saving measure, these were done away with and replaced with plain wood panels. Primary access throughout the first-class accommodations was via this staircase, which ran from Boat Deck to Main Deck. Small auxiliary staircases were also scattered throughout first class. The total for constructing and outfitting the entire main staircase was £15,300, which included the ornamental railings, screens, glass, and sliding gates to the lifts at a cost of £3,200.

The lifts in *Lusitania*'s first-class entrance caused a great deal of concern to everyone involved. Initially, she was to have only one passenger lift with an occupancy of eight people. As the design progressed, it was felt that two lifts was a better choice, but there was still quite a bit of disagreement about where they should be located. At first, the lifts were to be placed in the middle of the staircase well, but at a meeting of the shipbuilding sub-committee held in Clydebank on 26 January 1906, James Miller 'was in attendance and spoke very strongly against the proposal of putting the passenger lifts in the well of the Main Stairway'. Miller thought that they should be moved to either side of the entrance. The shipbuilder suggested that they be moved to the 'centre of ship near main stairway', but this proposal was rejected by Cunard. After many weeks of discussion, all the while looking at various designs and the relative expense of each proposal, Cunard had its final say on 13 March 1906 and decided that 'the Lifts were to be in the Well of the Main Staircase, and that no further discussion need take place on this point'.

During construction, there was a vigorous debate between Cunard and James Miller over the installation of a cloak room just outside the Dining Saloon on Upper Deck. Miller felt that passengers should have an enclosed room to leave their wraps and coats during meals, but Cunard didn't see the need for the extra expense. 'Mr Miller was of [the] opinion that the Cloak Room should remain and be fitted with a metal rack up centre, with numbered hooks all round... He was also of the opinion that by taking away the front of the Cloak Room, the Architectural scheme would be interfered with.' Unfortunately, Cunard won, and the cloak room was eliminated, leaving only a few plain recessed alcoves with several dozen hooks.

The pair of open shell doors seen in *fig.28* led to the first-class entrance foyer on E Deck. The lowest first-class deck, it was here that a major interior modification to *Lusitania* was made. The liner turned out to be so popular with the more influential segment of the traveling public that many third-class cabins just forward of this entry foyer were removed during an early refit, and the space was converted into first-class cabins.

First-Class Smoking Room

Decorated in an eighteenth-century style, *Lusitania's* first-class Smoking Room was paneled in finely figured Italian walnut, the beautifully grained woodwork and simple carvings giving the room a unique, more masculine flavor, which was quite different from the rest of the liner.

In August, 1906, James Miller's original plans for the room were rejected by the company because they were not considered 'sufficiently attractive for the Smoke Room of this ship'. By the end of that same month, Miller had revised his plans, and after re-submitting them to the Cunard board, they were accepted.

The large decorative fireplace at the forward end of the room burned coal, the only functional fireplace on board. The coal scuttle sits to the right, and the low metal barrier in front prevented hot coals from tumbling out of the fireplace and onto the carpet. The other fireplaces on board were simply architectural blanks put in place to ensure continuity of style. The smoke from this fireplace vented out of the ship through the fourth funnel.

As was customary on all British liners, the Smoking Room was an exclusive male preserve. So ingrained was this fact that Virginia Clark, a first-class passenger on board *Titanic*, would not enter that ship's Smoking Room to tell her husband that the liner had struck an iceberg.

First-Class Verandah Café

Originally calling for an enclosed café aft on Promenade Deck, the plans for *Lusitania* were modified in October 1905, and the idea of the café was done away with. This left nothing but an open area with tables and chairs and no side or aft bulkheads to enclose it, leaving it exposed to the weather. As late in the construction as June, 1906, this space was still simply a covered area. As the fitting out progressed, a skylight was added 'in the event of it being considered desirable later on, to cover in the space altogether for a café or other public room'.

Cunard obviously gave this a great deal of consideration, and after thinking better of leaving the sides of the room open, on 9 February 1907, they made the decision to modify the existing plans and enclose the room, leaving only the aft end open. A few ideas were suggested by Cunard as to exactly how they wanted the side bulkheads built, and among these was folding teak screens. This, however, would cost about £50 more than simply building steel bulkheads, and the folding-screen idea was vetoed. In the end, the total cost to outfit the Verandah Café including the furniture, skylight, and electric lighting was about £1,100.

Over the years, a number of alterations were made to the Verandah Café in order to bring it more in line with what was being offered on the newer competing White Star and German liners. Removable screens were added to the aft end so the room could be enclosed and used in all types of weather. Several years later, Cunard considered giving the Verandah Café a much-needed overhaul. The initial plan called for turning the café into a gymnasium, and this would have been a perfect conversion because the location of the room made it easily accessible by both first- and second-class passengers. The cost of the alterations was probably the deciding factor, and in January, 1914, Cunard rejected the gymnasium idea and settled on simply changing the décor. Rather than rowing machines, stationery bicycles, and mechanical camels, hanging plants, wicker, and trellis work were fitted, giving the newly decorated room the feeling of an outdoor café. The upgrade cost £580.

Forward on Promenade Deck was a small observation corridor from which passengers could look out over the bow even in the roughest of weather conditions. On early general arrangement plans, this area is shown as an observation room. As the design developed, the idea of a room was done away with, two additional cabins were put in, and only this passageway remained. This modest space with four portholes was the inspiration for the forward observation bars found on so many later liners.

In January, 1907, it was noticed during a regular inspection of *Lusitania* by Cunard's General Superintendent that the fore-and-aft passageways on *Lusitania* 'looked very narrow'. Upon further investigation, it was found that the corridors 'were not of the width originally arranged,' which was 4ft, and that the corridors on Boat Deck, Upper Deck, and the aft end of Promenade Deck were constructed at only 3ft 6in wide. The mistake evidently came about when figures on plans that were not intended to be used for construction were mistakenly transferred to construction plans.

Upon learning of the problem, Cunard immediately demanded to know how John Brown intended to remedy the situation. The builder submitted plans showing how the width of the corridors could be increased. On 30 January 1907, it was reported that John Brown had taken the matter in hand and proceeded to widen the Promenade Deck passageways to 3ft 11in. By the time Cunard's directors visited Clydebank on 9 February, most of the reconstruction on the other decks had also been completed. In the end, the width of *Lusitania*'s first-class passageways varied from 3ft 6in to 4ft 6in.

The first-class Barber Shop on *Lusitania* was located on the starboard side at the aft end of the first-class Promenade Deck, just forward of the second-class deck house. This upper-deck location was chosen to take advantage of the abundance of natural light. Two chairs were supposed to be fitted, but Cunard decided that one was sufficient. ' The second-class Barber Shop was of similar design and was located on Upper Deck aft.

Second Class

The second-class accommodations aboard *Lusitania* were placed in a separate deck house near the stern and were laid out vertically, one room above the other. There were four rooms available to second-class passengers – a Lounge, a Smoking Room, a Ladies' Drawing Room, and a Dining Room. In an innovative move for the time, Cunard asked *Lusitania*'s interior architect, James Miller, to consult on the decoration of these areas. On earlier liners, the rooms in the lower classes were left to the staff at the shipyard to design and outfit in a plain, simple fashion, but Cunard wanted something more for *Lusitania*. Miller and Robert Whyte, John Brown's resident architect, achieved something rarely seen on a liner, spacious inviting rooms for a 'lower class' of passenger.

Located on Boat Deck, the second-class Lounge was fitted out in mahogany by Waring & Gillow with easy chairs, settees, and tables dotting the room. As originally designed, the Lounge had open balustrades surrounding the staircase, which descended from the center of the room. A decorative skylight above allowed in plenty of natural light.

Unfortunately, a serious problem came to light during *Lusitania*'s trials: vibration. The severe shaking that manifested itself during her test runs must have thrown John Brown and Cunard into a near panic. What were they to do? They had just built the largest, fastest, and most technologically advanced liner of her day, and her second-class areas were nearly unlivable. *Lusitania* was immediately returned to the builder's yard, where a massive strengthening of her stern was undertaken. These two photos show the Lounge after the substantial rebuilding. Although still attractive, the room now boasted huge arched stiffeners, which broke up the Lounge and gave it a heavier, darker feel than before.

As with many of the first-class public spaces, the second-class Dining Room was decorated in the Georgian style with hand-carved details and mouldings, the rich mahogany furniture offsetting the room's white walls. The chairs, identical to those in first class, were spring loaded to face them away from the table when not in use. This saved the waiters the trouble of keeping them neat. This view was taken after the refit as evidenced by the pillar plunging through the center of the open well. Although the fare was simpler in second class than in first, the food was supplied by the same galley. In the mornings, shortly after breakfast, Catholic services were held here.

As with the first-class Dining Room, the style chosen for this feminine retreat was Louis XVI. A color scheme of gray and rose offset the beautiful satinwood furniture and gave the space a distinctly feminine feel. It was supplied with writing desks and two bookcases so that it served not only as a lounge but also as a writing room and library. As part of the alterations to reduce vibration, a large H-shaped settee was installed in the center of the room, effectively destroying the original design and doing away with much of the free-standing furniture.

A large room by the standard of the day, *Lusitania*'s second-class Dining Room was able to seat 260 at a time, necessitating two sittings for each meal. Because just over 600 people booked second-class passage on *Lusitania*'s final voyage, more than 140 over her designed capacity, the balcony of the Dining Room was used as an auxiliary dining area and was set with tables and chairs. Note the strengthening beams which nearly obscure the dome overhead. As with so many other changes in second class, this was done with an eye toward reducing vibration. A mahogany piano, inlaid with satinwood, was placed on the upper level of the room so that the orchestra could entertain passengers during meals. The photo below shows the same area above on the wreck today. The rectangular opening in the foreground is where the pillar in front of the piano once stood.

Just across the second-class entrance from the Ladies' Room was the Smoking Room. Decorated in a similar style to the Lounge above on Boat Deck, solid mahogany paneling offset the white plasterwork of the dome. In an interesting throwback to earlier Cunarders, wood decking and runners rather than wall-to-wall carpeting was installed.

One of only three pieces of artwork in public areas on the liner, this mosaic panel at the forward end of the Smoking Room depicts a river scene in Brittany. Art had never been a key decorative feature of early transatlantic liners, but with the advent of *Aquitania* in 1914, Cunard's interior designers entered a new phase of including large-scale pieces of art as focal points of the public rooms.

Above: The second-class main staircase ran from Boat Deck down to Main Deck. Just above this vestibule, at the head of the stairs on Boat Deck, was the second-class Lounge. To the left was the entrance to the Ladies' Room, and around the staircase to the right was the second-class Smoking Room. That some light fixtures are still not installed shows that this rare photo was taken while *Lusitania* was still under construction.

Right: Decorated in shades of light rose, dark rose, or green, *Lusitania*'s second-class cabins accommodated from two to four passengers. Each was fitted with a fold-up mahogany washbasin, complete with Cunard logos in the porcelain bowl and soap holders. Underneath were cabinets for the storage of chamber pots. Beautifully woven cotton bed covers and soft wool taffeta curtains complete the décor. Notice the circular moulding on the sideboard of each bed. The easiest way to distinguish a second-class cabin on *Lusitania* from one on *Mauretania* is the presence of this moulding. If it's there, it's *Lusitania*. If not, it's *Mauretania*.

Third Class

Located in the forward end of the ship, third class on *Lusitania* consisted of only three relatively modest-sized public rooms – the Dining Room, Smoking Room, and General Room – all of which were decorated in the same plain style. Fitting out of the third-class areas was nearly completed by the end of March, 1907. One interesting note is that much was made in the contemporary press about the third-class enclosed promenade on Shelter Deck. Installed along the outboard edge of this area were wooden seats, and this was considered a great improvement over previous liners in that 'the third-class passengers cannot be considered to be cabined and confined even in bad weather.'

Decorated in simple polished pine, the third-class Dining Room was able to accommodate only 350 passengers at a time. Because of the large number of third class carried, however, each meal in the Dining Room was served in two sittings. If the passenger load were especially full, the General Room and Smoking Room on Shelter Deck above were pressed into service as dining rooms, giving a total seating capacity of 550 per sitting or 1,100 per meal. The Dining Room also doubled as the main lounge for third class, and impromptu concerts and entertainments were often held here. To that end, an oak piano was supplied at a cost of £46, compared to the £179 for the piano in the first-class Lounge. Taken before *Lusitania* left John Brown, this photo shows the Dining Room tables set with dishes from the shipyard dining hall.

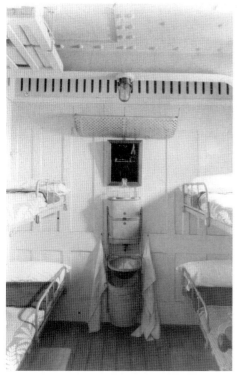

Above: The third-class Smoking Room set for dinner. When converted to an auxiliary dining room, the seating capacity was 108, but when used as a lounge, many more passengers could be accommodated because of the slatted benches along the outboard bulkhead. In the aft port corner of the room was a pantry, from which the food was served, and situated next to it was a serving station. Note the flare of the hull on the right-hand side of the photo. Just above this room is the forecastle, and on the opposite side of the ship was the General Room. A folding Bostwick gate, rather than doors, was installed at the entrance, probably to improve ventilation throughout the third-class spaces.

Left: The majority of third-class passengers on *Lusitania* were accommodated in two-, four-, or six-berth rooms. Only four cabins were fitted for eight people. This was an enormous advance over the large dormitory spaces on many of her contemporaries. As constructed, *Lusitania*'s third class could carry 1,186 passengers, but this was later decreased because of various modifications to the first-class accommodations on E Deck.

This cabin, J-29, is one of the better third-class rooms on board. Located on the starboard side of Main Deck, it was outfitted with a simple metal washbasin, a mirror, and a catch-all above. A single overhead light fixture was installed, and this stateroom had the 'luxury' of a porthole to provide natural light. No wardrobes or chests were provided in third-class cabins, and the lifejackets were stored in racks above the upper berths.

Lusitania's original plans called for a motorized launch to be placed on either side of Boat Deck, but 'as the ship is well sub-divided and propelled by four sets of turbine engines, the steam launches [need] not [be] fitted, as they involve weight, upkeep, etc.'

1. Just after the beginning of the twentieth century, Cunard's board of directors voted to construct a new company headquarters in Liverpool. Patterned after the Farnese Palace in Rome, the building overlooked the Prince's Landing Stage and was designed by Willink & Thicknesse in conjunction with Mewès & Davis. To give an idea of the immense size of their new headquarters, a book published by Cunard shortly after the completion of the building in 1916 stated that 'allowing each person comfortable standing room, it would be possible…to accommodate practically 250,000 people' in floor space that totaled over 450,000sq.ft, or nearly 11 acres.

2. A superb painting of *Lusitania*'s launch.

3. *Lusitania* arrives in New York after a late 1907 crossing. (Painting copyright © 1994 by Ken Marschall. Original painting, author's collection)

WOVEN IN SILK.

R.M.S. LUSITANIA.

Length 790 ft.   Breadth 88 ft.   Depth 60 ft.   Displacement 45,000 tons.

4. A beautiful silk post card of *Lusitania*, sent during her first two months of service. The hand-written message reads: 'I feel pretty shaky. No more of this boat for me!'

5. *Above:* A passenger list from the return maiden voyage of *Lusitania*, New York to Liverpool, 21 September 1907. Among those on board were Frederick McMurtry, Frederick Stark Pearson, and Mabel Pearson. All three perished on *Lusitania*'s final crossing seven and a half years later.

6. *Right:* A lovely second-class menu from *Lusitania*'s maiden voyage, showing the Drawing Room of *Carmania* and *Caronia*. The tops of most second-class menus were detachable post cards that could be sent to friends back home to show the luxuries found on board Cunarders.

Drawing Room: CUNARD R.M.S. "CARMANIA" & "CARONIA"

SECOND CABIN.

R.M.S. "LUSITANIA."

SUNDAY, SEPTEMBER 22nd, 1907.

MENU.

Hodge Podge

Boiled Salmon, Cucumber, Parsley Sauce

Mutton Pot Pie   Macaroni au Gratin

Roast Beef, Baked Potatoes
Boiled Turkey, Bechamel Sauce
Baked Ham, St. James

Dressed Cabbage   Carrots a la Crème
Boiled Rice   Boiled Potatoes

Apricot Tart   Gelee au Vin Oporto   Genoise Fancies
Plum Pudding, Sweet Sauce

Ice Cream

Cheese   Dessert

Tea   Coffee

7 and 8. Only a few color renderings of *Lusitania*'s interiors have ever come to light, but here are two examples. Above is the first-class Smoking Room and, below, the Verandah Café. Although color photography had been invented by 1907, no color photos of *Lusitania* seem to exist.

9. *Above:* An unusually rare stock certificate for the Leavitt Lusitania Salvage Co. Inc. This was issued by the first company that proposed to conduct 'serious' salvage on the sunken liner.

10. *Left:* Although the idea of a memorial to the sinking had been proposed shortly after the disaster, nothing came of the idea because of the war. Some preparatory work was done in the 1920s, and after many years of indecision, the monument was finally begun in earnest around 1933. More delays ensued, and the memorial was not completed until nearly four decades later.

11. Every year until his death, *Lusitania* survivor Walter Storch sent money to Cunard's Queenstown office requesting that flowers be placed on the three mass graves on the anniversary of the disaster. Seen here is one of the new markers erected in 1986.

12. With underwater visibility at the site between 20-40ft, only through an artist's brush can we see the entire wreck at once. The ship was in reasonably good condition at least as late as the mid-1960s, but it is unknown when the liner collapsed. Plainly visible are the remains of the liner's four towering funnels, which have long since crumbled into masses of rusted metal. Numerous davits, ventilators, and other easily recognizable items dot the debris field. (Painting copyright © 1993 by Ken Marschall. Original painting, author's collection)

13. During the 1993 expedition, the two-man submersible *Delta* examines the starboard anchor. Note the massive damage to the forefoot, caused when the liner hit bottom. (Painting copyright © 1993 by Ken Marschall. Original painting, author's collection)

14. In 1982, three of the liner's propellers were blasted from their shafts using plastic explosives. Two of them still exist, but the unfortunate third propeller was melted down in 1990 and turned into 'commemorative' golf clubs. Called 'The *Lusitania* Legacy', they sold for $9,000 per set, and one ad declared: 'The *Lusitania*…would be proud to see her damaged propeller transformed into a stunning set of clubs.' The director of the company that produced the clubs said of them: 'We looked into a couple of other things – fireguards for fireplaces with a relief of the *Lusitania* on them, and miniature boats – but golf clubs have a universal appeal. We could have made tacky souvenirs, I guess.' (Photo courtesy of Richard Woods)

15. The decorative bronze scrollwork from the port stern lying on the deck of the salvage vessel *Archimedes*. The scroll from the starboard side still remains on the wreck.

16. Among the recovered items were several hundred watch cases that were being shipped as cargo. A lone salvaged spoon rests against the bulkhead.

17. A selection of *Lusitania* dinnerware. Known by collectors as the 'spider web' pattern, this china was produced by Wedgwood and was used in her first-class Dining Room for only about a year before her loss.

18. Although dozens of pieces of china were recovered from the wreck in 1982, only a single example of this second-class pattern was salvaged. Because of a lack of basic conservation, by 1990 much of the china had deteriorated to a point where it simply fell apart in one's hands. These photos show a second-class milk jug shortly after its recovery (left) and the same piece, now without its handle, less than eight years later (right).

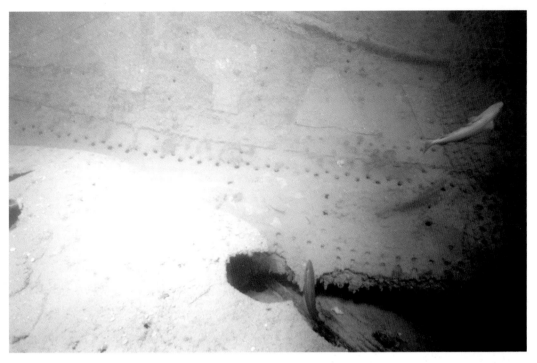

19. A close-up of the 'I-T-A-N' from 'Lusitania' on the port bow. Despite what had been reported by previous divers, the letters of the liner's name remain firmly attached to the wreck. A number of large corrosion holes were seen just above the name, and it was these openings that made past divers believe the name had been removed by the Admiralty to conceal the wreck's identity.

20. A pair of bollards and a capstan on the port forward side of the forecastle.

21. This pair of bollards is located in the starboard aft corner of the forecastle, the hemp mooring line still coiled around them just as *Lusitania*'s seamen left it nearly 100 years ago. The small piece of plating behind them is all that remains of the liner's bridge front. These same bollards can be seen in the photo on page 70. (Photo by Leigh Bishop)

22. One of *Lusitania*'s telemotors lying in the remains of her bridge. In the center of the photo just beyond the telemotor is one of two 'tell-tale' indicators that showed which direction the turbines were running. (Photo by Leigh Bishop)

23. The steam whistles on *Lusitania* were controlled by hand from the bridge through a pulley-and-rope arrangement. The original configuration was a single-chime whistle on each of the two forward funnels. The whistle on the first funnel was replaced with a double chime and then a triple chime. Seen here is one of the domes of the triple-chime whistle, and just behind is a second dome half buried in the bottom amid the rusted debris of the funnel. (Photo by Leigh Bishop)

24. This single-chime whistle from the second funnel remained with the ship her entire career and was salvaged in 1982.

25. An amazing photo of the only known window on the wreck with an intact pane of glass. That the glass survives in one piece is remarkable when one considers the massive destruction surrounding it. It was originally located on the port side of Boat Deck and opened into a first-class cabin. (Photo by Leigh Bishop)

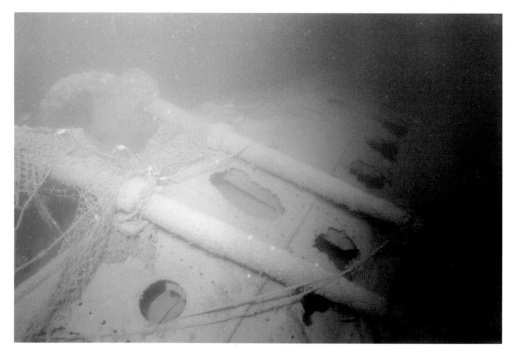

26. Seen here are two of the three davits that remain attached to the wreck. The porthole in the foreground looked into an athwartship passageway. The large eroded hole between the davits was the position of one of the portholes for cabin B-38.

27. The remains of a mosaic-tile bathroom floor on Promenade Deck just forward of the first funnel. Prior to the exploration of the wreck, only educated guesses could be made as to what these floors looked like. The drain and the foundations for the bathroom walls are still in place. (Photo by Leigh Bishop)

28. The double doors to the first-class entrance on E Deck. When the ship flattened, the decks were pressed tight against the hull, and the debris seen just inside the door is what remains of E Deck. The passengers' view upon entering the ship through these doors can be seen in the photo on page 51.

29. This view of *Lusitania*'s bilge keel was taken slightly forward of the break in the hull, which is just out of frame to the right. Despite ninety years on the bottom, there is relatively little growth on the hull, and the red anti-fouling paint can still be seen in many places under the waterline. The black on the ocean bottom is coal that spilled out when the ship broke in half.

30. A diver examines two of *Lusitania*'s telegraphs. The one on the left was a wall-mounted unit originally fitted in the aft wheelhouse under the docking bridge. The other was a free-standing pedestal unit located on the docking bridge above. In the background on the right is the docking bridge itself, which landed upside down when the ship collapsed. (Photo by Leigh Bishop)

FOUR

THE FINAL
FAREWELL

At the outbreak of the First World War in August of 1914, many British liners were withdrawn from commercial service and placed at the disposal of the Admiralty. By the spring of 1915, *Lusitania* remained the only large British liner offering regularly scheduled passenger sailings between Liverpool and the United States. Since the outbreak of hostilities, passenger revenue was down sharply, and to cut overhead, Cunard decided to shut down one of *Lusitania*'s four boiler rooms. This not only saved the cost of coal but also reduced the number of crew necessary to fire the boilers. The unfortunate consequence of this, however, was a decrease in her maximum speed from 26 to 21 knots.

On 1 May 1915, *Lusitania* departed New York for the final time, and by a strange twist of fate, her passenger list on this voyage was the fullest since the outbreak of war nine months before. This mostly had to do with a recent reduction of fares in an effort to attract more passengers, but even with the higher number of travelers, Cunard was only just about breaking even. The morning of her last sailing, a chilling warning issued by the Imperial German Embassy in Washington appeared in many New York newspapers. It read:

NOTICE!
Travellers intending to embark on the Atlantic voyage are reminded that a state of war exists between Germany and her allies and Great Britain and her allies; that the zone of war includes the waters adjacent to the British Isles; that in accordance with formal notice given by the Imperial German Government, vessels flying the flag of Great Britain, or of any of her allies, are liable to destruction on those waters and that travellers sailing in the war zone on ships of Great Britain do so at their own risk.

Imperial German Embassy,
Washington, DC, April 22, 1915

Many of her passengers, however, didn't see the notice, and those who did merely scoffed at it, thinking it another empty German threat. After all, they thought, what civilized country would dare torpedo an unarmed passenger liner carrying women and children?

The Cunarder was scheduled to sail at 10 a.m., but that morning a number of passengers were transferred from the Anchor liner *Cameronia* to *Lusitania*, delaying her departure. By 12:30, *Lusitania* was ready to sail. From high up on the top of Pier 54, a lone cameraman caught the entire departure on film. As the longshoremen let go *Lusitania*'s lines, a trio of tugs took over and pushed her slowly back into the river. After pointing the liner down stream, the tugs sounded their whistles, and Captain William Turner ordered his vessel slow ahead.

As *Lusitania* made her way out into the Atlantic, she was met by three British warships patrolling off the American coast. One of these was the Cunarder *Caronia*, which had been taken over by the Admiralty and had mounted guns shortly after the outbreak of hostilities, transforming the vessel into an armed merchant cruiser. When the warships approached, *Lusitania* slowed to a stop. A boat from *Caronia* was lowered and slowly made her way over to the great liner. After a short while, the lifeboat pulled away from *Lusitania*'s side, and she began her final trip across the Atlantic.

A boat drill of sorts was held every morning *Lusitania* was at sea, but only one lifeboat was involved, either No.13 or No.14, depending on which way the wind was blowing. The 'drill'

This is one of the few photos that shows *Lusitania*'s name on the lifeboats clearly enough to prove that each name was painted on and not attached as a brass plaque. The dark stripe running athwartship across the deck is one of *Lusitania*'s two expansion joints which allowed some 'play' in the superstructure, making it more flexible in heavy seas.

consisted of nothing more than eight or nine crewmen lining up at the boat, and upon the command of the officer in charge, climbing in and tying on their lifejackets. At the officer's order, the crew would climb out, remove their lifebelts, and return to their regular duties. It was described by one American survivor as 'a pitiable exhibition.' As a precaution, at 5:30 a.m. on the morning of 6 May, *Lusitania*'s lifeboats were swung out although they were not lowered to deck level nor were the snubbing chains removed.

As *Lusitania* neared the Irish coast, passengers discussed the possibility of the ship being torpedoed, but several survivors later recalled there was no great sense of alarm. That final evening all outboard lights were extinguished, and the shades in the passenger saloons and cabins were drawn. Despite the liner having entered the declared war zone, various activities on board went ahead as normal, including two charity concerts which raised badly needed money for seamen's charities in both Liverpool and New York.

When the morning of 7 May dawned, *Lusitania*'s last day of life began. She had only a few hours to live.

An interesting view looking aft on *Lusitania*'s Boat Deck, taken while she was anchored just outside of Queenstown Harbor. This shot dates to very shortly after the *Titanic* disaster as evidenced by the collapsible boats as well as the additional rigid boats that are not yet under davits. One boat is swung out clearly showing the collapsible underneath. Cunard altered *Lusitania*'s post-1912 lifeboat arrangement many times before her sinking, and as configured on her final voyage, she carried twenty-two regular boats and twenty-six collapsibles.

A picture of maritime perfection. *Lusitania* slices through the Irish Sea just off the Old Head of Kinsale in 1911.

Lusitania's superb Promenade Deck, looking aft. While at sea, passengers relaxed here in deck chairs and took tea as they watched the ocean pass by. With the addition of extra lifeboats after the *Titanic* disaster, this became the main promenade space for first class. Had *Lusitania* survived the war, the forward end of this deck probably would have been enclosed with a glass screen as was done on board *Mauretania* in the early 1920s.

Taken in the summer of 1914, this is one of only two known archival photographs of *Lusitania's* forecastle which shows a gun mount installed. It is located on the left-hand side under the coil of rope. Photos from the wreck also clearly show this feature. However, there is presently no photographic evidence to suggest that any of her other proposed gun mounts were ever installed.

Three bells of different sizes were fitted on board. They were located in the crow's nest, just above the bridge, and at the aft end of the second-class superstructure. The 10in bell seen here above the bridge is the only one which was engraved with the ship's name. The bollards next to the superstructure remain on the wreck to this day, and can be seen in *fig.21*.

An unusual view of *Lusitania* coaling early in her career.

A rare snapshot of some *Lusitania* crew members, showing the ship's name on the lifering. Taken under the aft docking bridge, the shed of Pier 56 can be clearly seen in the background.

A series of unusual *Lusitania* stereo-view cards was produced shortly after she entered service. This one was taken from near the top of the mast while docked in New York. A lifeboat is swung out for maintenance, and the liner has been warped away from the dock to allow barges in for coaling. Two other views in this series were taken from the same position, one looking directly down onto the forecastle and one looking down on the forward end of the superstructure.

1 August 1914. *Lusitania* is docked at Cunard's Pier 54 in New York just three days before Great Britain declared war on Germany. After she sailed on 4 August, paint crews were put to work during the voyage repainting the funnels and superstructure 'war-grey.' Many of the alterations made to the ship during her career are clearly evident in this picture. Also, note the extension of the pier to accommodate Cunard's new *Aquitania*, which had entered service just two months before the declaration of war.

Opposite: The only two known photos of *Lusitania* being repainted during her first crossing of the war. Taken while at sea, these superb images clearly show the camouflage scheme. *Lusitania* was repainted in her peacetime colors in November 1914, but by the time of her final voyage she was again camouflaged.

An excellent portrait of *Lusitania* in New York Harbor. The caption on the back of the original photo states that this is her final voyage, but the evidence in the photo shows that it can't be. Judging from the lifeboat arrangement and the brown stripe of paint just below Promenade Deck, this photo probably dates to late 1914.

This photo was taken during *Lusitania*'s final completed voyage from Liverpool to New York in April, 1915. Lifeboat drill is in progress and is being conducted by the officer on deck. A drill was held every morning the ship was at sea, but only one lifeboat was involved, either No.13 or No.14, depending on which way the wind was blowing. This boat is No.14. Despite the seriousness of this training, it consisted of little more than a few crew members climbing into the boat, tying on their lifejackets, and manning the oars. At the officer's order, they climbed out of the boat, and the exercise was over. The lifeboat drill during the final crossing was later described by one survivor as 'a pitiable exhibition.'

FIVE

DEATH OF INNOCENCE

On the morning of Friday, 7 May, after an uneventful week at sea, passengers on board *Lusitania* woke to a sound that no one on an ocean voyage likes to hear – that of the ship's fog horn. As the Cunarder approached Ireland, an intermittent fog bank settled around her, forcing Captain Turner to reduce the ship's speed to 15 knots. By 10 a.m., the fog had lifted, giving way to a glorious clear spring day, and Turner increased the liner's speed to 18 knots. There was a palpable sense of anticipation among the passengers when the Irish coast came into view. The voyage was nearly complete, and they would soon be home. Unknown to anyone on board, however, twenty-two ships had been sunk by submarines in the war zone during the six days since *Lusitania* sailed from New York.

At 1:20, Kapitän-Leutnant Walther Schwieger of the German submarine U-20 spotted at a distance of about thirteen miles a sight that must have made his heart jump. As he recorded in his log: 'Starboard ahead four funnels and two masts of a steamer with course at right angles to us...'. He couldn't believe his luck. Quickly submerging and traveling at its full underwater speed of 9 knots, the U-20 made a desperate attempt to get in position for a clear bow shot. After a tense twenty minutes, Schwieger had almost given up hope of catching the huge liner. She was steaming away from the U-20 toward the Irish coast so quickly that any chance of getting close enough for a clean shot was disappearing. Incredibly, at 1:40, *Lusitania* made a surprising turn to starboard, which would bring her directly across the bow of the still-submerged U-boat and in line for a textbook attack.

Half an hour later, at 2:10, with *Lusitania* nearly directly ahead and only 700 meters distant, Schwieger fired a single Type 'G' torpedo. In his war diary, he matter-of-factly recorded this history-changing event:

Torpedo hits starboard right behind the bridge. An unusually heavy explosion takes place with a very strong explosion cloud (cloud reaches far beyond front funnel). The explosion of the torpedo must have been followed by a second one (boiler or coal or powder?). The superstructure right above the point of impact and the bridge are torn asunder, fire breaks out, and smoke envelops the high bridge. The ship stops immediately and heels over to starboard very quickly, immersing simultaneously at the bow. It appears as if the ship were going to capsize very shortly. Great confusion ensues on board; the boats are made clear and some of them are lowered to the water. In doing so great confusion must have reigned; some boats, full to capacity, are lowered, rushed from above, touched the water with either stem or stern first and founder immediately. On the port side fewer boats are made clear than on the starboard side on account of the ship's list. The ship blows off [steam]; on the bow the name '*Lusitania*' becomes visible in golden letters. The funnels were painted black, no flag was set astern. Ship was running twenty knots. Since it seems as if the steamer will keep above water only a short time, we dived to a depth of twenty-four metres and ran out to sea. It would have been impossible for me, anyhow, to fire a second torpedo into this crowd of people struggling to save their lives.' [Translation from *The* Lusitania *Disaster* by Thomas A. Bailey and Paul B. Ryan]

In an instant, the lives of nearly 2,000 people had changed forever.

The exact point of impact has never been positively ascertained although Schwieger, the only witness with a clear, unobstructed view of the event, stated in his logbook that the torpedo struck just behind the bridge. Schwieger, as well as most survivors, later recalled that a second,

KEN MARSCHALL

1 May 1915. After a dreary, overcast morning, the sun breaks through the clouds as *Lusitania* departs Pier 54 for the final time. Despite an all-out war in Europe and a warning published in many newspapers by the Imperial German Embassy, most passengers seemed blissfully unaware that anything untoward might occur. Overseeing the hectic departure from the relative calm of the starboard bridge wing, Captain Turner watches as the tugs wait for his order to push *Lusitania's* bow downstream. A few interested spectators witness the historic sailing, not knowing that in six days, the liner will be lying on the bottom of the Atlantic. As a final gesture of farewell, *Lusitania* sounds her steam whistle. From the top of Pier 54, a lone cameraman films the departure. (Painting copyright © 1990 by Ken Marshall. Original painting, author's collection.)

Taken from the Cunarder *Caronia*, this is the last-known photo of *Lusitania* as she increased speed for her voyage home. Shortly after sailing, *Lusitania* was met by three British warships just outside the territorial limit of the United States. One of these was *Caronia* which had been requisitioned by the Admiralty for war service. Mrs David Loynd, a second-class passenger on *Lusitania's* final voyage, wrote a letter home to her sister during the crossing, in which she described the meeting. It reads, in part:

...there was a large warship in the distance English, and another on the other side of us, with the English flag flying. Then we stopped and we found there was another right beside us, so we stopped and talked with each other and put up different flags. It was a Cruiser. They said it was the Caronia, one of our English boats that has been taken for the War. It was painted a kind of dusky grey, nearly black. We found that the Lusitania has been painted a different colour. The Funnels are black, and the boat where it was white is now dark grey, this is so the enemy will not know her.

77

more-powerful blast quickly followed the first. To this day, its origin has not been satisfactorily explained although many theories – some plausible and some not – have been advanced.

Within seconds, the liner took a 15-degree list to starboard. This quickly increased to 25 degrees and showed little signs of stopping. In a brief eighteen minutes, the great liner disappeared from view with a loss of about 1,200 innocent passengers and crew. The sinking shocked the world and was the first incident in a long series of events that contributed to the ultimate entry of the United States into the First World War on the side of the Allies.

UNTERSEEBOOT 20 (U-20)

Built at the Kaiserliche Werft in Danzig, the U-20 was ordered on 25 November 1910 and launched on 18 December 1912, one of four submarines in this class. She was commissioned on 5 August 1913, and during her three-year career, she became a very successful hunter, mainly through the skill of her second and last captain, Walther Schwieger. The U-20 sank thirty-six vessels (excluding warships) for a total of over 144,000 tons. Despite these impressive numbers, U-20 is best known for her sinking of *Lusitania*.

On 4 November 1916, the U-20 ran aground near Harboøre, Denmark. After an unsuccessful attempt to refloat her, the crew abandoned the submarine and detonated torpedoes in her tubes to ensure that she did not fall into enemy hands. Because the sub was a hazard to navigation, in 1918, the Danish authorities sold the wreck to a salvager for 12,000 Kroner, who resold it in 1921 to Claus Sorensen for 2,500 Kroner. Sorensen salvaged what he felt was of value and planned to blow up the remainder of the wreck. In August, 1925, while crowds of curious Danes gathered to watch the spectacle, divers placed nine mines around the wreck. At precisely 12 noon, the mines were detonated. The U-20 was blown to pieces, but this did not entirely clear the wreckage.

After additional salvage in the mid-1950s and further demolition, the location of the wreck was forgotten. In 1979 a search for the remains of the U-20 began, and some wreckage was located, including the conning tower. The searchers returned in March, 1980, for a more thorough examination. By this time, few recognizable items were left, but a number of important artifacts were retrieved, including the conning tower, and are on display at the Strandingsmuseum St George in Thorsminde, Denmark. Today, what is left of the U-20 lies 450ft from shore in only 15ft of water.

Shortly after her grounding, visitors to the wreck of the U-20 posed for this photograph. Note the damage to the bow. (Photo courtesy of the Strandingsmuseum St George)

Although in an advanced state of decay, the wreck of the U-20 still attracted a large number of tourists. Here, the conning tower is still standing, but after the partial demolition of the submarine in 1925, it became detached and was later found on the bottom a short distance from the wreck. (Photo courtesy of the Strandings museum St George)

Above: In 1925, a partially successful attempt was made to remove the U-20 from its shallow sandbank because the wreck was deemed to be a hazard to shipping by the Danish authorities. Nine 70kg mines were placed around the ship and detonated by salvagers. (Photo courtesy of the Strandingsmuseum St George.)

Left: Shortly after 2 p.m., Schwieger fired a single torpedo at his target. Able seaman Leslie Morton was on duty as an extra lookout on the bow. At the British Inquiry, he testified:

At 10 minutes past 2 I looked at my watch and putting it into my pocket, I glanced round the starboard side and as roughly as I could judge, I saw a big burst of foam about 500 yards away four points on the starboard bow. Immediately after I saw a thin streak of foam making for the ship at a rapid speed… I turned round to [my mate] and said, 'They have got us this time.'

SIX

'THAT
TERRIBLE
DAY'

R ather than try to paint a picture of what it was like on that distant May afternoon, it seems best to let the survivors speak for themselves. Following are three unpublished accounts, one from a passenger of each class. It is hoped that these stories will help give a better understanding of those terrifying eighteen minutes.

Charles Bowring
First Class

14/5/15

My dearest girl,

Really it is hard to express to you how I feel & with what thankfulness I now write. I have indeed to thank God for sparing me & I can assure you when I got on the trawler I uttered a very heartfelt prayer of thankfulness that I was spared to see you dear girl & the kids.

It is hard at times not to believe that it is not one awful dream. When one thinks of the number gone, all of whom had someone who they loved or were loved by & are now no more, it makes one wonder why I was saved & others probably more worthy or more needed [are] gone. It is all one hideous nightmare & the horror of it cannot be described. You must have been on board & seen the number of helpless women & children absolutely struck down, murdered without warning, to realize what it all meant. It is too horrible to think about much less write. Words fail to describe one's feelings in regard to the perpetrators of such a damnable crime, wanton murder without warning & no effort to help or assist. Any nation guilty of such a dastardly crime must surely suffer in the long run.

I will try to tell you shortly my experiences, but I must wait until I see you, dear girl, for my brain refuses to work when I try to give a connected story.

The awful feeling, even when on the steam trawler four hours after the sinking [and] when told we couldn't get to Queenstown for another four hours [and] that you had heard the news & I could get no news to you for hours, was awful to contemplate.

We had had a splendid passage, calm as possible. Met quite a few nice people, alas mostly gone. And sighted land about 11.00 Friday morning, foggy before that but bright & sunny from then on.

I was at lunch when [I heard] a damnable concentrated thud. My first thought was they have got us & I went out of the saloon to [the] companion way. The explosion was close to where I was sitting on [the] starboard side (I thought first I was sitting on port side) [of] D deck at McCubbin's table. Only two at [the] table, Miss Paynter and self, were saved out of six. The explosion broke the ports & I saw the column of water so the [torpedo] must have hit us just by [the] elevators almost exactly amidships. There was, of course, a crowd rushing up [the] companion way, excited but no panic & no jostling. Dr McDermott – you remember him on [the] *Caronia* – was in [the] companion way telling everybody to keep calm & all would be well.

I got to B deck & went to my cabin & got two life belts & then went up on A deck port side. They [sic] was an enormous crowd [and] seemed to me mostly steerage passengers. [There was] fearful excitement but no panic. Sailors [were] in the boats, which had been swung outboard [the] day before, & [were] helping the women & children in. I gave the two life belts to two women & then saw Mr & Miss Paynter, who Fred Bush telephoned me about. She had her life belt on but wrong & I fastened it properly.

Charles Warren Bowring, First Class (Photo courtesy of Julie Bowring, author's collection)

Everybody was yelling women & children first & the first boat, bar the crew, had no one else as far as I saw. I helped to push her off [and] noticed the bow was going down quicker than [the] stern & turned round to see what was happening. The sailor who was looking after the stern fall tried to lower quicker & threw off a bight from [the] cleat. He lost control & the stern went down with a rush leaving [the] boat perpendicularly suspended by the bow & as I looked over [the] side, everybody was being tumbled out. I turned to look at what was happening to [the] 2nd boat & thought it was all right when suddenly it went down with a bang right on top of those in water out of first boat. I then made up my mind that I could do most good by getting as many life belts as possible & I went down to B deck again & got two out of a stateroom & picked up one in [the] passageway.

I got up to A deck & tried to get out on [the] port side, but she had listed badly & [a] jerk threw me out [the] starboard door on this side which was then getting very close to [the] water. There were very few people. I only saw one woman to whom I gave [a] life belt. A man grabbed another & I put on third. I saw she was then doomed & soon & kicked off my shoes & jumped in not more than five or ten feet. I made for a life boat but saw she was not clear & the davits were falling into her & so I swam away from the boat. I looked back & thought I was caught by [the] second funnel but cleared that & then thought [the] third had got me, but I just cleared it [by] it seemed like inches.

She sank by the bow but was turning on her starboard side & went down that way. I don't think I actually saw the last of her as I was trying to swim clear. It was exactly eighteen minutes from [the] time torpedo struck us until she disappeared. This is vouched for by the keeper at Old Head of Kinsale. We were about 10/15 miles S.W. from the Head.

I swam to a flat-bottomed boat & scrambled [on], helped by a steward on top. The canvas cover was still on, and we ripped this up & tried to put up the canvas sides. We found, however, on opening her, that the bow was stove in & we were only kept afloat by her tanks or watertight sides. Oars were got out, but she was water logged & we could do nothing.

By this time we had hauled aboard four women & about ten men. She looked as if she would sink under us, but, providentially, an upturned flat boat floated by & we fastened her to our boat & moved the women & part of the men including myself over. She was flush with the water & we stood on her for 3½ hours [with] water washing over our ankles. The girl I was holding on to I thought would pass away. She had only a jacket on & got almost black with cold & shock. We were practically helpless but managed to get two more women off some wreckage & three men who were drifting by on our two pieces of wreckage.

There was nothing in sight & we simply waited for something to turn up. After three hours we saw a motor life boat pick up some people a mile from us & then saw a number of smokes coming from Queenstown way. My watch stopped at 2.29 & a man on the trawler *Bluebell* told me it was 6 o'clock when they picked us up. Two torpedo boats arrived first, but they took people far away from us. It was perfectly calm luckily for if there had been any sea we could not have held on & only those few who got away in life boats would have been saved. Only five life boats proper floated upright, but some people were saved on upturned ones.

The only saloon passenger in our lot was a Mrs Osborne, of Hamilton, Ontario, (whose mother lives in Birkenhead) & self. She is a cousin of Mr David Binghams. I cannot tell you how strongly I feel about the way the naval reserve men on the *Bluebell* behaved. (She was armed, one of the patrol fleet.) They were splendid [in] the way they worked over some of the people they picked up – two women apparently dead. They revived one, a Lady Mackworth who one of the torpedo boat's dinghies brought to us. She was sitting in a cane chair supported by her life jacket unconscious when they took her from the water. Her father D.R. [sic] Thomas was also saved. The sight on the trawler was awful – three or four women more dead than alive, three men absolutely crazy & about 15 bodies of men & women & poor little kiddies.

It took us four hours to get back to Queenstown & we had to wait an hour while another trawler was landing survivors & bodies. We did not get ashore until nearly twelve. Bluejackets helped or carried everyone. Oh, they were fine & so wrought up with the perpetrators of such a cowardly unnecessary crime. I immediately cabled you & mother & I only hope you got same soon. I got your reply just as I was leaving Queenstown [at] 3 p.m. Saturday afternoon, which relieved me not a little as I knew the cables were blocked & as we were some of the last landed there were an awful lot of cables ahead of mine.

On the pier I saw Miss Paynter looking for her father; so I took charge of her & Mrs Osborne. Got Mrs Osborne to an hotel & stayed up with Miss Paynter looking for her father. I found his body next morning & had to break the news to her, poor girl. She was plucky, but oh, the sadness of it all. Fred Burl's other two friends, Mr & Mrs Dredge are both gone. A Mrs Popham Lobb, a friend of Teddy Darrell's, was saved & I had her also under my wing to Holyhead.

Saturday morning was awful as I was looking for two friends of Mrs Osborne & trying to overcome red tape regarding Mr Paynter's body, which I succeeded in getting off on [the] same train as we left. The bodies were in three different places & coming in all the time & I tried to identify those I knew for the sake of their families. It was an awful job, but one could not think of self under the circumstances.

Coming back, I had Mrs Osborne, Miss Paynter, and Mrs Lobb under my charge. I must confess crossing the Channel from Dublin to Holyhead I was in a blue funk & we sat on deck in pitch darkness with life belts under our feet. Mrs Lobb I put in [sic] train at Holyhead for London & Mrs o/ & Miss P. [were] both going near Birkenhead. We arrived at Chester at 2 a.m., both ladies being met there & George Wilson & Frank meeting me there. Henry's car met us at the landing stage & we arrived at [illegible] at 4 a.m. Mother & Ethel were up. Both had an anxious time having only got my wire at 7 a.m. Saturday.

I was all right on Sunday but must confess my nerves were pretty well on edge & knowing this, had to keep quiet. Everybody is kindness itself & all ask after you & worry over your anxiety. I have had about a hundred cables & letters from old friends & your friends here. Received a letter this a.m. from Celia M. Taite. She is the only one I can't trace. Cable from Stett, W. Price, Ed Brown, Baylies, Teddy Darrell, practically all the staff at B. & Co. & numerous others.

I will come back on an American boat as you wish, but there is nothing between *New York* tomorrow & *St Louis* on [the] 29th. They are safe & so are others as I don't believe those Huns even would have the frightfulness to do more. I, of course, saved nothing & have to get a complete outfit. Everything [is] gone including my small picture of you & the post card group of you & the kids. This week is wasted as I was in no condition to start in to replenish, but today I am fine & will probably go up to London on Monday. Please don't worry & believe me I can't get back one minute too soon. Edgar will probably come back on [the] same boat.

How are you & the kiddies? Please kiss them for me & ask them to do the same to you for me. It will seem ages before I get back to you, but I am very thankful I am spared to see you all again. A very heartfelt prayer went up when I got on board the trawler & realized I was saved & able to see you in the near future once again. I can't express half the thankfulness I feel & the hope of seeing you, dear girl, very shortly is always with me.
Good night dearest & all love possible from

Yours always,

Charlie

Please excuse this rambling epistle, but I can't possibly write all I feel & words fail me of love & thankfulness for everything.

Avis Dolphin
Second Class

Waverley Hotel Sackville Street, Dublin.
Monday, May 10.

My dearest mother,
I hope you are all well. I am just splendid. I will tell you everything from the time we got on the
boat till now. The first day I was not at all sick, but for three days I was sick. The third day I was
laying in the lounge room, and a gentleman came up there and was sitting very near to where I
was laying. He asked me if I was quite comfortable. He said it wasn't possible to be so he went
out and came back with a pillow wrapped up in a shawl. He then asked me if I wanted anything
– fruit or tea. I said no. So after a while Hilda asked if I wanted anything, but I wasn't at all hungry
so she went out and Mr Holbourn went out and asked her if I would like a deck chair. She said I
would so while I was there he told me all about his children. He has three, the old is seven years.
He then went for tea and after tea I felt so very much better we went to a concert in the second
class dining room. Then the next night we went to a concert in the first class lounge room.
    Mr Holbourn has 13 or 14 Shetland ponies. His summer home is in the Shetland Islands. In
the winter in Edinburgh. He has travelled nearly all over the world. He is a great lecturer. In
the morning he told me a lot of things about boats that will interest Jack. Suddenly the boat
took a great turn and was dodging zig-zag here and there.
    We had our dinner second sitting, and we were eating our dinner when 2 torpedoes struck
the ship, and we were on the opposite side to where it was struck. Mr Holbourn said to wait
till the rush got out. Then we had to go up one flight of stairs to the deck, and Mr Holbourn's
cabin was on that floor so he went in there and got three life belts. He put one on me and put
one on Hilda and tried to force Miss Smith to take one, but she wouldn't because she said he
had a wife and three children. So he put it on himself. He put us all on a lifeboat, but a lot of
men jumped in on top of us, and that broke one of the strings. The boat was let down dry, and
we were all in the water. Then I lost sight of Hilda & Miss Smith. I was under water for about a
minute then floated around for a few seconds. I saw a string. I got hold of it, and I found it was
a raft. They pulled men on and then we got a lot of ladies and gentlemen on our boat. The men
had knives. They cut off the canvas and pulled up the sides of the boat and started rowing the
boat. Then I stood up and exercised a little and got warm. Then one of the gentlemen that was
rowing spoke to me, and I found his name was Mr Colebrook. He was by himself. He said he
would look after me so then we saw a lot of torpedo boats. There were twenty sent out on guard.
We saw twelve. There was one sail boat very near us. We rowed to it and they were dragging
a boat with about five men in it. So all the ladies got in there and the gentlemen stayed in the
other boat and were towed along too. After a while a small steamer with one funnel came up
and asked us if we wanted to get in there. So we said yes and we all got in there and there was
a lovely fire going. There was hot brandy and tea to drink. I had tea then I went in one of the
cabins and took off all my wet cloths and put a rug around me but I couldn't get my clothes
near the fire to dry them. Then I saw a lady with just a towel to keep her warm so I gave her
the rug I had and I took the towel. Then one lady asked me to get under her rugs and so I did.
Then we had something to eat. Then I lay down and covered up with her rug. As it was a large
one, it covered us both up. Then after a while I put my wet things on again. (There were lots of
ladies that had their babies torn away from them by the suction of the water. The boat was 12
mins. going down.) When I was dressed, the boat had landed at Queenstown and [I] went to the
Queen's Hotel and first of all cabled to you and Auntie Louie. There were 80 survivors taken to
the Queen's Hotel and others to other hotels. There I found that Mr Holbourn was there. When

Avis Gertrude Dolphin, Second Class
(Photo courtesy of Avis Dolphin Foley,
author's collection)

I got into bed they brought up some hot milk and it was lovely. In the morning Mr Holbourn couldn't get up. Because he was not able to, Mr Colebrook took me up town and I got a pair of shoes and a hat for I had lost mine. I lost everything except the things I had on when I left home. In the afternoon Mr Holbourn got up and he went out to get clothes for himself. The Cunard provide everything for us. That night we went to a show and on Sunday we started for Dublin and arrived last night. We are now at a rather nice hotel. We start to-morrow for England by boat. I had a bath this morning and washed my hair for whenever I touched the scalp my hands got filthy. I can't find anything of Hilda and Miss Smith. There was a Helen Smith and another Miss Smith but we couldn't find out who they were. We gave your address and Mr Holbourn's father's address if they were found, and the Cunard people would let you know.

I escaped very nicely. A few bruises is all I have and can't feel those unless I press them very hard. I haven't got a cold or anything. The *Lusitania* was carrying the most passengers it ever did. There were two thousand one hundred and ninety-eight people (2,198), not counting crew. The Captain had signals three times not to take the usual course but as he thought he knew most he went his own way. Even the German warned him. His name was Turner. He was saved. There is one gentleman Mr Holbourn knew was in the water for four hours. There were hardly any first or third class passengers saved. It was a very terrible thing.

There was one very rich man [who] offered Mr Holbourn money but as he had money he did not take it. So he asked Mr Holbourn of anyone who lost all their money and he said I had lost mine so he gave me all I had lost.

I guess I had better stop now. Mr Holbourn is going to take me to have my eyes tested again and we must see him at 2 o'clock. It is now one and we have to have dinner.

Give my love to all and will write again soon.

Your loving daughter,

Avis xxx

Francis Frankum
Third Class

'I Went Down on the Lusitania' by F.J. Frankum

Fifty years ago, on 7th May 1915, the Cunard liner R.M.S. Lusitania, a luxury liner of 32,500 tons was torpedoed and sunk by a German submarine off the Old Head of Kinsale, Southern Ireland, while on a voyage from New York to Liverpool. The liner sank in 20 minutes with the loss of 1142 lives. A survivor, who was a schoolboy at the time, tells of his experience and rescue.

I first saw the light of day in a little wooden house in London, Ontario, Canada, under the shades of the Maple Leaf. My parents had emigrated from England a few years earlier. Father was a humble carpenter from Hampshire, seeking his fortune in the Dominion.

With the approach of the industrial 'slump', mother and I journied [sic] to England for a short season while father remained to face the trials and troubles of unemployment with countless others in similar circumstances.

While still an infant, I returned to Canada with my mother, and on the voyage across the Atlantic our ship struck an iceberg. We were transferred to an icebreaker and continued our journey safely to shore. Thus early was I introduced to the perils of the sea.

Conditions having improved, father decided to remove to the States, and we found our way to Detroit. Here he purchased a small 'lot' of ground in a growing suburb, and, being a joiner with building contracting experience, he planned to build a home for us. I well remember, when about four years of age, visiting the plot and seeking where he had laid the foundations of our future home. It was not long before he had a four-apartment bungalow built for us, and we had at last a home of our very own, with a flagpole in the front garden over which fluttered the 'Stars and Stripes'.

The district was a growing community and Church activity was very small, so my parents started a Sunday School in our house, which was well attended by the boys and girls of the neighborhood. So much so, that in due course official recognition was made of the effort, by the building of a little wooden church nearby, where father had charge of the children's work.

A younger brother and sister were my home companions. Memories still linger in my mind of the happy times we had together – of the fun we had in the long grass near our home; of the digging of a well for water; of the tornado which swept the country and left our house standing while others nearby were blown to the ground; of the heavy snow in winter, when father built a snow house complete with an American stove inside and a chimney through the roof; and of the pleasant sails on the steamer 'Belle Isle.'

Then came the Great War. The call of the Home Country was strong, and my parents felt they would like to see the Old Folks again. In due course their minds were made up and passages were booked on the Cunard Liner 'Lusitania', at the time one of the luxury ships of the Atlantic. Our little cottage was sold. We watched our belongings being packed into boxes and crates, and sent ahead to be placed on board. The day of our departure eventually arrived, and we took farewell of our 'home'. Friends came to the station to see us off, and crossing the Detroit river in the train ferry we were soon on our way. The long train journey was very interesting to us children.

Arriving in due course in New York, we made our way through the sheds at the quayside to the giant liner lying alongside. I remember how impressive the ship appeared as we walked up the gangway and on board. We were shewn to our cabin and settled down. Then we put to sea.

The first few days of life at sea were uneventful. My mother was an accomplished pianist, and was asked to play the piano for a concert in the Third-class cabin in aid of Seamen's Charities.

Francis J. Frankum (left) and his father Joseph, Third Class. (Photo courtesy of Margaret Frankum, author's collection.)

Sports were held on deck, and I was successful in winning a race and obtaining a pocket-knife as a reward.

Friday 7th May 1915, found the liner steaming along on a smooth sea in bright sunshine off the south coast of Ireland. The coast could be seen on the horizon. Most of the 1,200 passengers were thinking of the approaching arrival at Liverpool where friends would be waiting to meet them with a cheery welcome. What a happy re-union many expected!

In the early afternoon we were resting in our cabin, when – without any warning whatever – a loud explosion suddenly shook the ship from stem to stern. A torpedoe [sic] had struck the vessel! She heeled over immediately. We knew what had happened, and at once made to get on deck. Father grabbed my brother in one arm and my young sister in the other, and we rushed for the stairway. The time was about 2 p.m. We made our way out into the sunshine and on to the sloping promenade deck. I recall, quite clearly, walking along the sloping deck and looking across to the other side of the ship where we should have seen the sky, but seeing instead the blue sea. Owing to the crush at some of the companion-ways, father decided to get on the boat deck by climbing over part of the superstructure. While doing so, and trying to hold the two children, he found my brother slip from his grasp and tumble six feet to the deck below, but happily without much harm. Eventually we reached the boat deck, but owing to the list of the liner very few boats could be launched. We made our way towards the stern and found there a lifeboat lying on the deck. Father thought that if we got into this boat, and the liner sank, it would float off and we would be safe. I remember seeing many people floating about in the ocean far below us.

Father placed us in the lifeboat, where there were also a few other people. Then kneeling down on the deck, he prayed for our safety, committing us to the care of God, and reminded us of the hymn we had learned and so often sung in our little Sunday School in Detroit – 'God Will Take Care of You.'

As we sat in our lifeboat, another explosion shook the ship and she began to sink faster. She had a sharp list to starboard and her bow was under water with the stern high up in the air. As she gradually slipped under we could see the water coming up round the funnels, until it began to pour down one funnel. Further and further she sank and the sea crept up to our lifeboat and we expected it to float off. And then, to the horror of all the occupants, the water came pouring in and the lifeboat went under also. It was fastened to the deck! Immediately we found ourselves in the water and were all separated. I had no lifebelt on and could not swim at all, but in some providential way, I clambered on to an upturned lifeboat.

The time was 2.20 p.m. In 20 minutes one of the world's luxury liners had gone to the bottom of the ocean, the victim of a cowardly U-boat attack, and with her over 1,000 passengers and crew.

The sun streamed down out of a clear sky on the scene. Wreckage, luggage, lifeboats, and drowned people floated all around, where the liner had once been.

I was safe on my upturned boat, and floated about on the surface of the ocean for several hours. I remember seeing a toy ball float by, similar to one I had had, and thinking it was mine. Fortunately the day was fine and the sea calm. Later in the afternoon rescue ships came on the scene, and in due course I was taken aboard a ship which had one funnel with a flag painted on the funnel – this memory is quite clear. I was taken below and given warm food and attention, while the ship cruised about for other survivors.

When darkness fell, and the mantle of night covered the scene, we made our way back to Queenstown harbour. There a sailor carried me on his back to a hotel for shelter and attention. Well I do recall the warm fire and the hot bread and milk provided by the kind hotel-keeper. I should like to meet him again. And then, I went to sleep hardly realizing the significance of the events of the past day.

What of my father? When the liner sank, he had been drawn down by the suction, clinging to mother trying to save her, until an underwater explosion separated them and he had to swim for the surface. When his breath had almost failed he reached fresh air and swam for some wreckage. Making his way to another upturned lifeboat he clambered on it and helped to pull others to safety. One young man on the same lifeboat, was in a very emotional sate, and promised that if we reached land safely, his life would be difference in future. This man saw a body drift by and said: 'I wonder who that is'. Taking an oar, he turned the body over, to discover it was his own father. A gun-boat came on the scene later on and they were taken on board. Father helped to render artificial respiration to some who were taken out of the water, as he had first-aid experience, and was able to be useful. He, too, found his way with the ship to Queenstown when night fell, and slept a troubled sleep wondered what had happened to his wife and family.

Next morning, he searched among the bodies brought ashore to see if he could trace his loved ones. Then he met another survivor whose acquaintance he had made on the liner. This man said that he thought he had seen me at the 'Rob Roy' hotel. Hardly daring to believe that this might be true, he hurriedly made his way there and dashing in asked if they had a boy there by the name of 'Frankum.' They said they had, and he was shewn into the bedroom where I lay in bed, to be greeted with the welcome 'Hullo Daddy, how did you get here?' He was overwhelmed with joy to know that, at least, he had one of his family left to him.

After getting some new clothing, we spent a day or two in Queenstown visiting the hospitals and mortuaries in an effort to trace the remainder of the family but without avail; they were seen no more but had shared the date of the 1,142 passengers and crew – innocent victims of the savagery of war – swelling the total of those who suffer by 'man's inhumanity to man'.

A few weeks later one of our trunks was washed ashore by the tide on the south coast of Ireland. This had our name painted on it and was returned to us, containing some of our

Sphere torpedo strike.

belongings. Today, I number among my treasured possessions several things in particular. One is the pocket knife which I won in a race on the deck of the liner, in my pocket when I went down. Another is my father's watch stopped at 2.20 p.m. when he entered the water, and still bearing the rust stains of the salt water. Another is the programme of the last concert held on board the night before the ship sank, bearing the names of my mother as pianist, and my father as one of the artistes. Finally, the old Stars and Stripes flag which flew over our American home, rescued from the box washed ashore, stained by the waters of the ocean but sill intact – a memory of the tragedy of half a century ago.

The Oliver Bernard Renderings

Oliver Bernard was born in London, England, to parents of a theatrical background. At an early age, he went to sea as a cabin boy and a seaman and later became assistant artist at the Royal Opera House at Covent Garden. In May, 1915, he sailed on *Lusitania*'s final voyage. On the afternoon of 7 May, he was standing at the starboard rail just outside the Verandah Café, deeply lost in thought, when a disturbance on the water caught his eye. Immediately realizing what it was, Bernard watched the lethal missile approach the liner.

Bernard survived the disaster, and following his arrival in London, he was found by a man from the *Illustrated London News*. The reporter asked Bernard 'to make a sketch of the disaster as he saw it happen.' Bernard declined and despite his protests, the young man begged for 'just pencil notes to show their own artist how to produce correct illustrations of what happened' and 'pushed some sheet of paper in front of [Bernard], cajoling him into making little scrawls with pencil, pen-and-ink blots, to explain his verbal account of how the *Lusitania* was hit and behaved thereafter...'.

'How did she go down?' asked the *ILN* reporter. Bernard looked at him somberly for a moment and then replied: 'Not a bit like the usual pictures of liners diving head first, propellers in the air, and all that stuff. Wouldn't have known she was sinking if it hadn't been for the way she listed...'. Finishing the drawings, Bernard handed them to the young reporter, who went away delighted with his Sunday morning's work.

Bernard later met with the art editor of the *ILN*, who insisted that he should come to their offices the next morning to see what was being produced with his sketches. Bernard 'called on the *Illustrated London News* as promised... The Editor treated him as an honoured visitor. They showed him his scribbles actually set up for the printer, two whole pages just as he did them; he was asked to add certain notes of description. The Editor produced some champagne, which encouraged [Bernard] to sit up and do what was required more cheerfully.'

After the *Lusitania* disaster, Bernard joined the army and became a commissioned officer in the Royal Engineers. He later returned to the theater and died at age 58 at St Thomas's Home in Lambeth, London, on 15 April 1939. He was cremated at Golder's Green on the eighteenth of that month.

The whereabouts of the sketches is unknown.

Column of water

2.22 pm
STARBOARD BOAT DECK

The last boat away from Starboard side (N 2)
just missing funnel.

DR — F. BERNARD

The great upheaval of water after the Lusitania went under

Oliver P. Bernad

"GONE" 2.30 pm

Left: In one of the most dramatic scenes of the sinking ever produced, *Lusitania* rolls over to starboard while passengers and crew struggle for their lives. It was estimated by survivors that her maximum list during the sinking was anywhere between 25 and 35 degrees. Shortly before the final plunge, *Lusitania* began to right herself, finally coming to rest on her starboard side.

Below: The aftermath.

Below: Seemingly unaware of the tragedy that had just unfolded, children in Queenstown play in their new-found 'toys'. A number of additional boats were washed ashore along the Irish coast in the weeks following the disaster and were sold to local residents.

SEVEN

CITY OF
THE DEAD

O n the evening of 7 May 1915, a grim parade of rescue ships arrived in Queenstown Harbor, bringing both the living and the dead from the third great passenger ship disaster of the new century. For the next few days, family members separated from one another during the chaos of the sinking, as well as relatives of those who had been on board, now searched the streets, hospitals, and makeshift morgues looking for any sign of their loved ones.

During the ensuing week, rescue ships reaped a grisly harvest off the south coast of Ireland. As an incentive to ensure that as many victims as possible were recovered, a reward was offered for each body found – £1 for an 'ordinary' body with the American government paying an additional £1 bonus if the body was identified as an American. The jackpot, however, would belong to the lucky soul who found the remains of Alfred Gwynne Vanderbilt, *Lusitania's* wealthiest passenger. The millionaire's family had offered £200 for his recovery, but even with this grand prize, his remains, if found, were never identified.

Digging the three huge graves in Clonmel Cemetery began two days following the disaster, and on 10 May, the first mass burial was held in Grave C. The interments at Clonmel then continued in not only the mass graves but also in numerous private plots until 16 June when three-year-old Alfred Scott Witherbee was laid to rest. For many months after the disaster, bereaved families of identified victims wrote to Cunard requesting that their loved ones be disinterred and sent home for burial. By mid-October, Cunard's main office in Liverpool tackled the question of the continual requests and wrote to their representative in Queenstown:

We are in receipt of your letter of 12th inst. with various enclosures regarding the exhumation of bodies buried in the public graves at Queenstown, all of which we have carefully read. Kindly allow us to say at once that your hands are perfectly free, and we have not compromised your position in any way. The Burial and Sanitary Authorities seem to have taken it for granted that out of consideration for the feelings of the friends of the overwhelming majority of the victims buried in these graves, you as joint custodians would see eye to eye with them and oppose any disturbance. They (the authorities) feel strongly on the matter, as you are already aware, and do not hesitate to say that the opening and closing of these graves and the disturbance of the coffins would be desecration.

To which Cunard Queenstown replied:

We are in receipt of your letter of the 14th inst. regarding our remarks in connection with the exhumation of bodies. We are glad to note that you have not compromised our position in any way, but it certainly was a surprise to us to learn from two sources, that we were strongly opposed to exhumation. We would not like it to go forth that we have no feeling for the friends of the overwhelming majority of the victims buried in these graves, by continually having same disturbed, but, as we have already pointed out, we must be diplomatic in all these cases, and when we have a request with reference to prominent American Citizens, it would not be policy for us to place any objection in their way. We do not by any means desire to encourage exhumation.

Immediately after the disaster, anyone with a German-sounding name became a possible target of the anti-German sentiment that swept through the UK. Riots broke out in the streets of many major cities, and crowds looted German-owned shops.

One of the final requests for exhumation was made in July of 1917 by the relatives of first-class passenger Elizabeth Seccombe, whose father had been a Cunard captain and under whom Captain Turner had served. The body of her brother Percy had also been recovered, but he had been cremated and returned to his family in New Hampshire right after the disaster. The request of the Seccombes was denied on the grounds that 'the removal would be detrimental to the public health.'

Above: Two horse-drawn hearses, carrying victims of the *Lusitania* sinking, leave Queenstown and begin their journey to Clonmel Cemetery. This heart-breaking procession slowly wended its way through the hills just outside the town where the police and military lined the funeral route.

Opposite above: Because of the large number of caskets that had to be transported to the cemetery, horses and carts from neighboring areas were brought in to help relieve the burden. Body numbers were chalked on the tops and sides of many of the caskets to help locate them later if the need arose.

Opposite below: The three mass graves were opened on Sunday, 9 May 1915, and were dug by local soldiers. The Royal Garrison Artillery supplied parties of twenty, under senior non-commissioned officers, to load the coffins onto the hearses that were met at the cemetery gate by sixty men of the 4th Irish Regiment. One hundred men of the same Irish regiment carried out the interments.

The confusion in Queenstown immediately following the disaster overwhelmed the authorities and especially the Cunard offices. With more than 760 survivors to attend to, not to mention hundreds of recovered victims, it was no wonder that mistakes were made. While attempting to determine what had become of some of the victims' bodies, it was realized that a few could not be accounted for. In an internal memo dated 9 July 1915, Cunard admitted that some of the recovered bodies were missing and that their most likely resting place was Grave C.

In the continuing effort to identify victims, the question came up several times as to why some bodies were not photographed. On 2 June 1915, Cunard Queenstown wrote the following to the Liverpool head office:

We are in receipt of your favor of 1st inst., and in reply can only assume that owing to the stupidity of the photographer no photograph was taken of No. 54, he apparently taking it for one of the bodies identified.

And then on 17 June 1915:

We are in receipt of your favor of 16th instant enclosing copy of letter received from Cockspur Street Office, and in reply beg to say that no bodies were buried before the evening of 10th May, and all identified bodies were supposed to have been photographed. As already explained, however, our photographer did not display much brilliancy, and it is quite possible that a body or two may have escaped his notice.

The mass *Lusitania* graves became a popular spot for soldiers and sailors to visit and pay their respects. On the first anniversary of the sinking, the Queenstown Urban District Council organized 'Decoration Day' with the cooperation of Cunard in remembrance of those who were lost.

The first and largest batch of *Lusitania* survivors arrived on three special trains at Euston Station in London between on 9 May. The arrivals numbered between sixty and seventy. Most survivors were too distraught to relate their experiences to the anxiously waiting public.

A post card of a recovered *Lusitania* lifeboat on display at Broadstairs. The sign above it reads:

Lusitania *Raft. This raft is one from the S.S.* Lusitania *torpedoed by a German submarine off the coast of Ireland May 7th 1915, [it] was washed ashore having several bodies aboard. Presented to the town June 7th 1917. Lest We Forget.*

This boat was used as a prop in numerous propaganda photos taken just after the sinking and is very likely the same boat referenced in the following memo from Cunard Queenstown to the main office in Liverpool: 'Referring cable from New York boat was capsized when floated into Schull and bodies of four women and three children were found underneath and in the vicinity…'. As late as 1949, the boat was still on display.

'The Sham Tribunal'

In what one well-known *Lusitania* historian has appropriately called 'The Sham Tribunal,' the British Government attempted to perform the ultimate damage control. Caught with their pants down, one of Britain's largest liners had sunk less than twenty minutes after being hit by a single torpedo. How could this have happened? But the question more important to the British Government was how could they shift the blame?

The British Inquiry into the loss of *Lusitania* began on 15 June 1915, five weeks after the tragedy. Presided over by Lord Mersey, who had 'performed' admirably at the *Titanic* and *Empress of Ireland* inquiries, the entire proceeding lasted less than a week. Very few witnesses were called to give evidence, and in some instances, they were hand-picked to make sure their facts shored up the 'official' version of the 'Hunnish crime.' Because Britain was at war, some of the more sensitive testimony, which consisted mostly of the Admiralty orders issued to Captain Turner and how and why he followed them the way he did, was held *in camera* and was not for public consumption. This *in camera* testimony was not made public until 1919.

It was by no means a probing inquiry like the two held after the loss of *Titanic* three years earlier. The American *Titanic* Inquiry ran for nearly 1,200 pages and was conducted over eighteen days. The British Inquiry was even more extensive, running thirty-six days during which more than 25,000 questions were asked. By comparison, the inquiry into the loss of *Lusitania* runs only 103 pages (including title pages and the index of witnesses) with a mere 2,312 questions having been asked.

Some information that eventually would prove useful to historians was uncovered during the inquiry, but not much. In the end, the only conclusion that could have been reached during the war by an inquiry held in the United Kingdom was handed down. The blame was placed squarely on the shoulders of the Imperial German Government and Walther Schwieger. To quote the court's decision:

> The Court, having carefully enquired into the circumstances of the above mentioned disaster, finds, that the loss of the said ship and lives was due to damage caused to the said ship by torpedoes fired by a submarine of German nationality whereby the ship sank.
>
> In the opinion of the Court the act was done not merely with the intention of sinking the ship, but also with the intention of destroying the lives of the people on board.
>
> The whole blame for the cruel destruction of life in this catastrophe must rest solely with those who plotted and with those who committed the crime.

Opposite below: A large number of lifeboats were either washed ashore or found floating near the disaster site. Throughout 1915 and 1916, the boats and their contents were sold off bit by bit. One lifeboat, for example, went to a doctor in Skibereen for £10. Two collapsible boats, on the other hand, sold for a mere £3. Two deck chairs sold for only 5 shillings. A number of people wrote to Cunard, asking if it were possible for them to keep as souvenirs the items they had found washed ashore. (Photo courtesy of Robert Forrest)

DERRICK HOISTS RECOVERED
TREASURE AND RECORDS TO
SURFACE

OPEN END
OF TUBE

FLOAT

MOTHER SHIP

MEN DESCEND
STAIRWAY WITHIN
FIVE-FOOT STEEL
TUBE, OPEN AT TOP

WORKING CHAMBER, WITH
AIR UNDER PRESSURE EQUAL
TO SEA'S, SERVES AS
DIVING BELL

AIR LOCK
ACCUSTOMS
DIVERS TO
SEA PRESSURE

DERRICK LIFTS
OUT CONTENTS
OF HOLD TO BE
HAULED TO
SURFACE

OBSERVATION
CHAMBER

SEARCH LIGHTS
ILLUMINATE INTERIOR
OF SHIP

DIVERS LEAVE
AND ENTER CHAMBER
THROUGH TRAPDOOR

SUNKEN LUSITANIA LIES
UPRIGHT WITH TOP DECK
UNDER 175 FEET OF WATER

One of the first serious discussions about finding, filming, and salvaging *Lusitania* came from
Simon Lake, who designed a device with which divers could reach the wreck using a staircase
enclosed in a metal tube. In 1931, Lake contracted with Paramount Pictures 'for exclusive motion
picture rights' to any film he took at the site because the film studio was considering making a film
about the disaster. A short time later, Paramount decided not to go ahead with the project. This
frustrated Lake because he felt 'that there is a great abundance of marvelous material in the sunken
Lusitania upon which to base a remarkable, thrilling, dramatic sea story.'

EIGHT

GIANT OF
THE DEEP

For twenty years after the sinking, the wreck of *Lusitania* remained undisturbed although she was certainly in people's thoughts – most of them treasure hunters. The first half-baked recovery schemes were launched within days of the sinking. Of course, nothing came of them because of the war, but as early as 1917, a London solicitor approached Cunard asking if his client should negotiate with Cunard or the Liverpool & London War Risks Insurance Association, Ltd., for possible purchase of the wreck. No details were given about what this anonymous purchaser intended to do with the wreck, and nothing came of this particular scheme, but by 1919 the first intent-to-salvage notice appeared. Then in the early 1920s, the Leavitt Lusitania Salvage Co. was formed. Its purpose, naturally, was to recover some of the treasure rumored to be aboard. For several years, plans were laid to begin salvage work, and stock was actually sold in the company, but as with every other salvage proposal, save one over sixty years later, this too faded into obscurity.

The wreck was identified in 1935 by a team from the Tritonia Corporation, using the research ship *Ophir* and a depth recorder. During the search, the depth recorder located an object that measured 780ft long and 84ft high. Even though no other wrecks off the south coast of Ireland could possibly fit this description, a diver by the name of Jim Jarratt descended to the mystery ship in an attempt to verify which it was. After being lowered, he walked around on the ship's side, becoming the first man to actually see the great lost liner since her sinking twenty years before. At a depth of 240ft, Jarratt said: 'I am standing on the plates of a ship; I can see her two-inch rivets. There is amazingly little sign of corrosion beneath the slime covering the hull.' After his quick dive, Jarratt was pulled to the surface, fully intending to revisit the wreck, but he never returned. In an odd twist, one of the crewmen of the *Ophir* was *Lusitania* survivor Robert Chisholm, her former second steward.

Because of building world tension, which eventually erupted into the Second World War, *Lusitania* remained largely forgotten and again faded into obscurity. During the late 1940s and early 1950s, however, gossip abounded on the south coast of Ireland that various ships of the Royal Navy had been moored over the wreck and had carried out extensive depth charging. One author even went so far as to say that he had located divers who admitted diving to the wreck during the given time frame, but firm evidence has not been produced to support the claims. The rumors continued.

After the discovery of the wreck in 1935, *Lusitania* lay silent for twenty-five years. With his first dive to the ship on 20 July 1960, John Light, an American diver from Massachusetts, opened a new chapter in the complex and intriguing history of the liner. On and off during the next few years, he and his crew made over 130 visits to the wreck – 42 of which were made personally by Light – despite poor conditions and primitive equipment. The number of dives becomes even more astonishing when one considers that the divers were breathing the only thing available to them at the time – compressed air. Mixed gases were not yet available and would have greatly extended bottom time and decreased the effects of nitrogen narcosis. The most interesting thing to come out of these descents to the wreck was the film Light brought back. Some people have simply dismissed the footage as 'worthless' – it is too dark and grainy, they say, and nothing can be learned from it. This could not be further from the truth. Despite the severe limitations of the time, John Light was able to capture on film a unique record of a moment in *Lusitania*'s history, which shows her in reasonably good condition despite her fifty years on the bottom. One just needs to know what one is looking at.

In 1935, Jim Jarrett became the first diver to visit the wreck. Here he is being lowered over the side of the support ship *Ophir*.

In 1967, Light purchased the wreck from the British War Risks Commission for the princely sum of £1,000 although the purchase price only included the 'hull and appurtenances.' With ownership of the wreck firmly in his hands, over the next two years, Light planned an extensive series of visits to the ship using newly developed diving technology with the hope of performing a complete survey of the wreck and perhaps discovering what caused her to sink. Unfortunately, in December of 1969, Light was forced to suspend his operations because of financial difficulties. He left Ireland and never returned although his research into *Lusitania* continued unabated until his death almost twenty-five years later.

Despite the impact the sinking had on history, the mystery surrounding her loss, and the relatively shallow depth of 300ft at which the wreck lies, *Lusitania* has been visited very infrequently over the years. Nearly two decades passed between the Light dives and the next visit in the summer of 1982 when a consortium, headed by Oceaneering, International, conducted a video survey of *Lusitania* using a surface vessel and a rather primitive ROV. On 10 September of the same year, Oceaneering's saturation divers began their work on the wreck, ostensibly to find out why she sank. It has been rumored, however, that the real reason for the dives was to recover items, such as the propellers, which could be sold for scrap and turn a quick profit. The operations lasted about six weeks until the support ship *Archimedes* returned to port because of bad weather. That winter, the company projected a return to *Lusitania* in 1983 to thoroughly document the contents of the No.2 cargo hold where the munitions were thought to have been stored. Because of legal entanglements in the Irish Courts over the ownership of the wreck, however, this was never carried out, and the wreck was again ignored for over ten years. Although Oceaneering and author Colin Simpson claimed that the vessel was lost because of the detonation of an illegal cargo of munitions, the company had declined repeatedly to make its documentation public, preventing independent analysis. Not surprisingly, Oceaneering now claims that all documents relating to their *Lusitania* dives have disappeared.

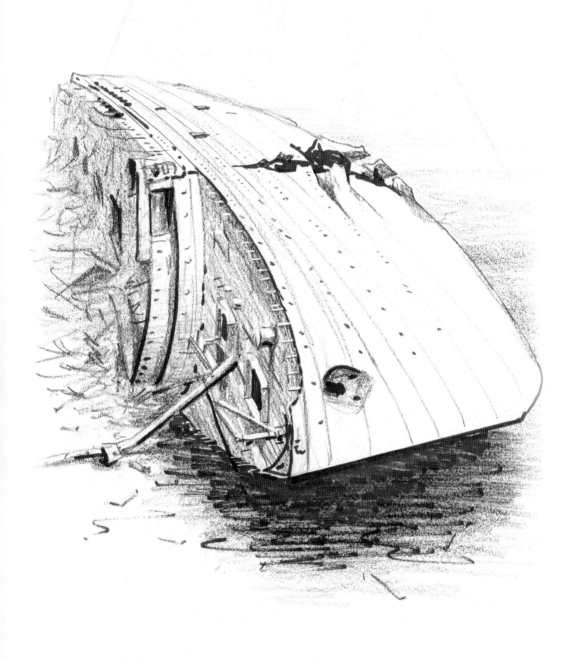

One of the finest items recovered during the Oceaneering salvage operations is this decorative window from the forward end of Boat Deck. Some white paint still clings to the frame, and the rubber gasket remains supple even after sixty-seven years on the bottom. This is the only window of this pattern salvaged and is presently in the author's collection. See *fig.25* for an identical window still on the wreck.

Opposite: Before the *Lusitania* expedition in 1993, a preliminary sketch was produced showing, rather optimistically, how historians expected the wreck to appear. The drawing was based on the best available evidence from prior expeditions, and no one expected the wreck to have deteriorated as far as it had. This rendering bears almost no resemblance to what was found. (Original sketch by Ken Marschall, author's collection)

One thing that did come out of the 1982 expedition was the recovery of a large number of exceptional artifacts, including the crow's nest bell, one of the ship's whistles, a docking telegraph, three propellers, portholes, windows, Cunard crockery and silver, and thousands of smaller items. Tragically, no conservation work of any kind was performed on these historic pieces, and a number suffered irreparable damage as a result of this lack of basic care. Among the most interesting artifacts brought to the surface were several hundred military fuses. Although it had been generally known since *Lusitania* left New York for the last time that she had been carrying illegal munitions, the fuses provided the first hard evidence.

On 31 May 1989, nearly seven years after their recovery, the first two of the salvaged pieces were placed on the auction block at Sotheby's of London. They were the two most historically significant artifacts recovered – the crow's nest bell and the single-chime steam whistle from the second funnel. Because the two items were last-minute additions to the auction, the prices realized were ridiculously low for such important artifacts, and Oceaneering decided against publicly auctioning the remaining pieces.

During a visit to Scotland in 1990, I examined the remaining artifacts first hand. Because of their great historic value, I rather innocently expected each item to be carefully packed, labeled, and stored but was shocked when the storage bins were opened. These priceless, historic pieces were thrown haphazardly into the shipping containers with no thought or care given to their well being. It was a miracle that some of the more fragile items survived intact.

Later that same year, Oceaneering contacted a select group of individuals and held a sealed-bid auction to sell off the artifacts that were still in their possession. Nearly all the available items were purchased during this sale. Afterwards, however, the pieces that had not been purchased were disposed of despite a flurry of desperate letters from concerned maritime historians who wanted to purchase them in an effort to save them for posterity.

In 1993 Robert Ballard, the man who found the wreck of *Titanic*, gathered together a group of experts in his own attempt to solve the riddle of why *Lusitania* sank. In accounts of the disaster, nearly all survivors agreed on at least one thing – that shortly after the detonation of the torpedo, there was a second, more thunderous explosion, the cause of which has never been satisfactorily explained. Upon hearing of the up-coming expedition, maritime historians were certain that, at long last, someone was going to give *Lusitania* the detailed attention she so well deserved. They had good reason to be hopeful. Unlike all the other wrecks Ballard has explored, the location of *Lusitania* was known long before the expedition began, saving many arduous days or even weeks of searching. She also lies in fairly shallow water, only about 300ft. It should have been like shooting fish in a barrel. Although some intriguing things were learned during the two-week exploration, the expedition fell far short of its stated goal for a variety of reasons. The mystery remained unsolved.

In the years since the 1993 expedition, a number of teams of scuba divers have visited the wreck to examine *Lusitania*'s remains more closely. Once again, although some remarkable footage was shot, no further clues have been brought to the surface that might help solve the mystery of why she sank. After a dive team visited the ship in 1994, the Irish Minister of Arts and Culture placed an Underwater Heritage Order on the wreck, which prohibits diving to or recovering artifacts from *Lusitania* without the sanction of the Irish authorities.

In the ninety years since her loss, *Lusitania* has closely guarded her secrets. Tides and currents have taken their toll, and except for the hull and some scattered fittings, little of the ship remains that is easily recognizable. What was once the largest and most magnificent creation of her day is now only a mass of contorted metal on the bottom of the Atlantic. High-tech expeditions have tried, but failed, to shed any light on her sudden tragic demise, and historians continue to debate over most aspects of her loss. Despite her poor condition, she still remains an impressive sight, 300ft down in a misty green haze, 11.2 miles off the Old Head of Kinsale.

Large sections of corroding superstructure were recovered in 1982. Still embedded in them were numerous windows like these, but by the time the artifacts went up for sale in 1990, only a single example of this pattern of window remained. The whereabouts of the others is unknown.

One of three propellers salvaged from the wreck. This one was purchased by the Merseyside Maritime Museum, and every year a service is held at the propeller in memory of those who perished in the sinking.

Appendix 1

Chronology

1902 – The first preliminary renderings are submitted depicting *Lusitania* and *Mauretania* with only three funnels and three propellers.

1902-1904 – Design of the new liners occupies two full years.

8 October 1905 – Lord Inverclyde, Cunard's chairman and the driving force behind the construction of *Lusitania* and *Mauretania*, dies aged forty-four.

7 June 1906 – Mary, Lady Inverclyde, widow of the former Cunard chairman who first envisioned the two Cunard flyers, launches *Lusitania*. In attendance are 600 official guests, but many thousands of 'uninvited' spectators witness the history-making event.

June 1907 – *Lusitania* departs the builder's yard for her journey down the Clyde.

27 July 1907 – At 8:50 p.m., *Lusitania* sails from the Tail o' the Bank for her trial trip around Ireland. Among the passengers for this voyage are Lord Pirrie and The Right Hon. A.M. Carlisle of Harland & Wolff; Mr William Watson, chairman of the Cunard Steamship Co.; Sir W. Forwood, Deputy Chairman of Cunard; Lord Inverclyde, son of the late Cunard chairman; Ernest H. Cunard, grandson of the line's founder; Alfred Booth; and the Hon. Charles Parsons, inventor of the turbine.

August 1907 – *Lusitania*'s formal trials are held. She reaches speeds in excess of 26 knots.

3 September 1907 – At anchor in the Mersey, *Lusitania* is open to the public, and in one day 10,000 people visit the new 'wonder ship.'

7 September 1907 – To the strains of *Rule Britannia*, *Lusitania* sails from Liverpool on her maiden voyage under the command of Captain James B. Watt. An estimated 200,000 people line the shore to watch the sailing.

12 September 1907 – In an attempt to draw the world's attention from *Lusitania*'s maiden voyage, Harland & Wolff announces the building of two new mammoth liners, which would become *Olympic* and *Titanic*.

13 September 1907 – *Lusitania* arrives in New York for the first time. Delayed by fog, she did not set a new record for the fastest Atlantic crossing. Her voyage lasts five days fifty-four minutes, and her average speed is 23.01 knots, missing the old record by less than thirty minutes.

October, 1907 – *Lusitania* crosses the Atlantic in four days nineteen hours and fifty-two minutes, winning back the Blue Riband for Britain and making her the fastest liner in the world. Some sources quote her average speed as 23.993 knots, but the official statement released by Cunard states that it is 24.002.

2 November 1907 – When *Lusitania* sails on her voyage from Liverpool to New York, she carries £2½ million in sovereigns and gold bars, making this the largest amount ever entrusted to one liner. The shipment is packed in 334 boxes and weighs 20 tons.

10 November 1908 – William Thomas Turner is appointed commander of *Lusitania* upon the retirement of James B. Watt. Turner joined Cunard in 1878 as third officer of the *Cherbourg*.

January, 1910 – During an exceptionally rough winter crossing, *Lusitania* encounters waves estimated at over 80ft high. One of these hits the ship with such force that the bridge front is pushed back several inches and a number of the forward lifeboats are reduced to matchsticks. The bridge floods to a depth of 5ft, and the wheel is torn from its telemotor. *Lusitania* is steered from her aft steering station until the wheel on the bridge can be reattached. The liner is withdrawn from service while repairs are undertaken.

Winter, 1912 – Because of the loss of *Titanic* the previous April, the number of lifeboats on *Lusitania* is permanently increased, giving her a lifeboat capacity which will accommodate everyone on board.

4 August 1914 – Britain declares war on Germany. During her first crossing of the war, *Lusitania*'s funnels are painted gray to help disguise her identity.

November, 1914 – Cunard reduces the number of crossings for *Lusitania* to one round-trip per month. The liner's No.4 boiler room is shut down to conserve coal and reduce overhead. This reduces her maximum speed from 25 to 21 knots. Her funnels are repainted traditional 'Cunard orange' as sign of confidence that the tide of war is turning in Britain's favor. Passage fares are lowered in an effort to increase passenger figures.

3 November 1914 – Britain declares the North Sea a military area and lays mine blockades.

4 February 1915 – Germany declares the waters around Britain a war zone. *Lusitania*'s funnels are painted black.

10 February 1915 – The Admiralty issues secret orders to merchant captains to ram or flee from hostile submarines.

22 April 1915 – The Imperial German Embassy in Washington D.C. issues a notice reminding the traveling public that 'a state of war exists between Germany… and Great Britain…' and that ships entering the war zone are liable to destruction. It is not published in the newspapers until the morning of 1 May.

30 April 1915 – The German submarine U-20 sails from the German Naval Base at Emden under the command of thirty-year-old Kapitän-Leutnant Walther Schwieger.

1 May 1915, 12:30 p.m. – *Lusitania* departs New York for the last time. She is delayed 2½ hours because of a last-minute transfer of some passengers from the *Cameronia*.

5 May 1915 – The U-20 sinks the 132-ton *Earl of Lathom* about ten miles off the Old Head of Kinsale.

6 May 1915 – Using gun fire and a single torpedo, the U-20 sinks the Harrison Line steamer *Candidate* about thirteen miles south of the Coningbeg Lightship. That afternoon, the U-20 sinks another Harrison Line vessel, the *Centurion*, with two torpedoes seventeen miles south of Coningbeg.

7 May 1915 – At 2:10 pm off the Old Head of Kinsale, Schwieger fires a single torpedo at *Lusitania*. She sinks in eighteen minutes.

8 May 1915 – John J. Horgan, the coroner in Kinsale, Ireland, begins a three-day hearing to determine guilt for the sinking. Naturally, it is placed on the Germans.

9 May 1915 – Digging of the three mass graves begins in Clonmel Cemetery, just outside of Queenstown. Each is 30ft long by 20ft wide.

10 May 1915 – The burials of the *Lusitania* dead begin. Seventy victims are placed in Mass Grave C, and the grave is then sealed.

22 May 1915 – The last burial is held in Mass Grave B. It holds fifty-two victims.

24 May 1915 – Mass Grave A is sealed. It holds twenty-three victims.

15 June 1915 – The British Inquiry into the sinking begins.

16 June 1915 – Three-year-old Alfred Scott Witherbee is laid to rest, the last victim to be buried in Clonmel Cemetery. Bodies of more victims continue to wash ashore until late July, but many are unidentifiable.

August 1915 – Cunard receives the first of three insurance payments from the Liverpool & London War Risks Insurance Association, Ltd., for the loss of *Lusitania*. The first payment totals £500,000.

19 August 1915 – The White Star liner *Arabic* is torpedoed by the German submarine U-24 some fifty miles southwest of the Old Head of Kinsale. She sinks in nine minutes with a loss of forty-four lives, two of whom are Americans.

30 August 1915 – Orders are issued to U-boat commanders to spare passenger ships.

4 September 1915 – Schwieger, still in command of the U-20, sinks the Allan liner *Hesperian* without warning. He is summoned to Berlin and severely reprimanded.

February, 1916 – The second installment payment due on the loss of *Lusitania* is received from the Liverpool and London War Risks Insurance Association, Ltd., in the amount of £240,333 6s 8d.

May, 1916 – Cunard receives the final insurance installment of £277,333 6s 8d for *Lusitania*.

7 May 1916 – On the first anniversary of the disaster, flags on all Cunard ships and offices fly at half mast.

4 November 1916 – The U-20 runs aground on the Danish coast. After fruitless attempts to refloat her, she is partially destroyed the following day when her crew detonates two torpedoes in her tubes.

1 January 1917 – The Cunard liner *Ivernia* is sunk in the Mediterranean while on trooping duties. Her captain is William T. Turner, who was in command of *Lusitania* when she was lost.

6 April 1917 – The United States declares war on the German Empire.

5 September 1917 – The German submarine U-88, now under the command of Walther Schwieger, former captain of the U-20, reportedly strikes a mine and sinks with the loss of all aboard.

23 August 1918 – Judge Julius M. Mayer, sitting in the Admiralty Branch of the United States District Court of New York, absolves the Cunard Line of all liability in the sinking of *Lusitania*, placing the blame solely on Germany.

11 November 1918 – The Armistice bringing the First World War to an end is signed.

23 June 1933 – Captain William Thomas Turner dies.

6 October 1935 – The wreck of *Lusitania* is located by the *Ophir*.

26 October 1935 – The *Ophir* anchors over the wreck, and a diver named Jim Jarratt descends to the liner. He becomes the first person to see her since the day she was lost. A memorial service is held at the site.

1953 – Divers incorrectly report that the wreck is lying on her port side. Some Irish fishermen also claim that the wreck is lying on an even keel.

20 July 1960 – In a feat remarkable for the time, American John Light makes his first of forty-two dives to the wreck, breathing nothing but compressed air. Over the next several years, he captures an amazing photographic record of *Lusitania* after forty-five years on the bottom.

1966 – John Light's final dive to the wreck.

1967 – John Light purchases the wreck from the British War Risks Association.

September-October, 1982 – Oceaneering International conducts the only known salvage operation on the wreck. Numerous items are recovered, and Ireland claims the artifacts as national treasures. After a lengthy court battle, an Irish court rules in favor of the salvagers.

1983 – Oceaneering plans to return to the wreck for further salvage. Because of legal entanglements this does not come to pass.

1989 – One of *Lusitania*'s salvaged propellers is purchased and placed on permanent exhibition at the Merseyside Maritime Museum, Liverpool, England.

31 May 1989 – The salvaged bell and whistle of *Lusitania* are auctioned at Sotheby's in London. The prices realized are well below expectations.

1990 – The second of the three salvaged propellers is melted down to produce 3,500 sets of commemorative golf clubs called 'The *Lusitania* Legacy'.

1990 – The remaining items recovered by Oceaneering are sold. Those not purchased are 'disposed of'.

August, 1993 – Dr Robert Ballard leads an expedition to the wreck.

June, 1994 – Polly Tapson expedition. This is the first time since John Light explored the wreck in the 1960s that free divers visit the site.

January, 1995 – The Irish Government places a Heritage Order on the wreck, which prohibits diving or salvage without the government's permission.

1996-2002 – Additional expeditions to the wreck by free divers.

Appendix 2
Cunard Liners Lost During the First World War

(Extracted from a memo dated 16 April 1920)

Ship	Tons	Date of loss	Gross Value	Book value at date of loss	Recovered from War Risks, etc.
Lusitania	30,396	7.5.15	1,681,050	1,036,883	1,000,000
Caria	3,031	6.11.15	19,179	10,219	17,506
Veria	3,228	8.12.15	44,798	7,443	(b) 30,479
Franconia	18,149	4.10.16	420,521	318,547	(a) 700,000
Alaunia	13,405	19.10.16	319,618	286,134	561,257
Ivernia	14,278	1.1.17	324,268	70,171	(a) 300,000
Lycia	2,715	11.2.17	13,407	5,192	60,000
Laconia	18,099	25.2.17	432,238	346,911	679,906
Folia	6,705	11.3.17	175,000	175,000	175,000
Thracia	2,891	27.3.17	15,910	6,182	67,000
Feltria	5,253	5.5.17	50,000	5,110	75,000
Ultonia	10,402	27.6.17	171,997	25,617	176,758
Volodia	5,689	21.8.17	160,000	60,332	180,000
Vinovia	5,503	19.12.17	190,000	36,057	160,000
Andania	13,405	27.1.18	320,469	264,939	(a) 605,000
Aurania	13,936	4.2.18	470,365	470,474	700,000
Valeria	5,865	21.3.18	160,000	58,604	164,000
Ausonia	8,152	30.5.18	122,050	83,697	(a) 285,000
Vandalia	7,333	9.6.18	215,000	55,604	(a) 270,000
Ascania	9,111	14.6.18	151,782	101,585	245,000
Carpathia	13,603	17.7.18	317,616	86,386	(a) 450,000
Flavia	9,291	24.8.18	180,000	25,778	250,000
(22 Ships)	220,440		5,955,268	(c) 3,536,865	7,151,906

(a) Amounts received direct from Government.
(b) £10,000 of this amount received from outside Brokers.

FIRST-CLASS CABIN ASSIGNMENTS FOR *LUSITANIA*'S FINAL VOYAGE

The following information was taken from the original Cunard berthing book for the 1 May 1915 sailing of *Lusitania* from New York to Liverpool. All names have been transcribed exactly as they were written in 1915, and known errors have not been corrected.

Cabin No.	Name	Ticket No.	Steward	Notes
A-001	Pierpoint, Mr Wm John	46100	Bond, Edward	
A-002	Staff Captain	n/a	Bond, Edward	Originally a passenger stateroom, cabin A-002 was reassigned to the Staff Captain upon creation of the post in 1912 following the *Titanic* disaster.
A-003	Padilla, Mr Frederico G.	46135	Bond, Edward	Duplicate ticket numbers were issued to Mr Frederico G. Padilla and Mr C.T. Brodrick.
A-004	Lassetter, Mrs H.B.	46107	Bond, Edward	
A-005	Lewin, Mr F. Guy	46156	Bond, Edward	Moved from D-041
A-006	Battersby, Mr James J.	46084	Bond, Edward	
A-007	Keeble, Mr and Mrs W.	10864	Randall, Charles	Moved from A-017
A-008	Boulton, Mr Harold, Jr.	20609	Bond, Edward	
A-009	Harris, Mr Dwight C.	46141	Bond, Edward	
A-010	Pope, Miss Theodate and	46015	Bond, Edward	Moved from D-054
A-010	Robinson, Miss Emily	46015	Bond, Edward	Moved from D-054
A-011	Schwarte, Mr August W.	46122	Bond, Edward	
A-012	Page, Mr J.H.	46103	Bond, Edward	
A-014	Lassetter, Mr F.	46107	Bond, Edward	
A-015	Dougall, Miss C.	46065	Bond, Edward	
A-016	Hodges, Mr and Mrs Wm S.	14677	Perry, John	
A-017	Bruno, Mr and Mrs H.A.	46146	Bond, Edward	Moved from A-007
A-018	Hodges, Master D.W.	14677	Perry, John	
A-018	Hodges, Master W.S., Jr.	14677	Perry, John	
A-019	Crichton, Mrs Wm	46088	Randall, Charles	
A-020	Naumann, Mr F.G.	46042	Perry, John	
A-021	de Ayala, Mr Julian	46077	Randall, Charles	
A-022 & bath	Baldwin, Mr and Mrs Harry B.	46056	Perry, John	
A-023 & bath	Kessler, Mr Geo. A.	46162	Randall, Charles	
A-024	Schwarcz, Mr Max M.	46114	Perry, John	

Cabin No.	Name	Ticket No.	Steward	Notes
A-025	Rogers, Mr and Mrs Frank A.	10859	Randall, Charles	
A-026	Moodie, Mr R.T.	46117	Perry, John	
A-027	Timmis, Mr R.J.	46118	Randall, Charles	
A-028	Munro, Mrs	6348	Perry, John	According to a ship's daily newspaper saved by third-class passenger Joseph Frankum, it was reported that Mrs Munro did not board *Lusitania* and missed the final sailing.
A-029	Withington, Mr Lothrop	1290	Randall, Charles	
A-030	Jenkins, Mr Francis B.	46137	Perry, John	
A-031	Partridge, Mr Frank	46058	Randall, Charles	
A-032	Letts, Mr Gerald A.	46139	Perry, John	
A-033	Miller, Capt. Jas B.	13431	Randall, Charles	
A-034	Stackhouse, Comdr J. Foster	46075	Perry, John	
B-001	Barnes, Mr Allan C.	6926	Morse, Robert	
B-001	Trumbull, Mr Isaac F.	8568	Morse, Robert	
B-002	Gibson, Mr Matthew	13432	Williams, William	
B-003	Rumble, Mr Thos W.	10870	Morse, Robert	
B-004	Buswell, Mr Peter	13429	Williams, William	
B-005	Lauriat, Mr Chas E., Jr.	1297	Morse, Robert	
B-006	Robinson, Mr and Mrs Chas E.	74681	Williams, William	
B-007	Emond, Mr W.A.	46148	Morse, Robert	
B-008	Scott, Mr A.J.	17108	Williams, William	
B-009	Knox, Mr S.M.	14679	Morse, Robert	
B-010	Stone, Mr Herbert S.	46069	Williams, William	
B-011	Keser, Mr and Mrs Harry J.	14678	Morse, Robert	
B-012	Phillips, Mr Wallace B.	46097	Williams, William	
B-014	King, Mr T.B.	46064	Williams, William	
B-015	Kempson, Mr M.	10869	Morse, Robert	
B-016	Leary, Mr Jas.	46063	Williams, William	
B-017	Wood, Mr Arthur	46110	Morse, Robert	
B-018	Plamondon, Mr and Mrs Chas A.	20697	Williams, William	
B-019	Not occupied	n/a	n/a	
B-020	Smith, Miss Jessie Taft	46143	Williams, William	Duplicate ticket numbers were issued to Jessie Taft Smith and Dr Owen Kenan.
B-021	Baker, Mr James	14674	Morse, Robert	
B-022	Tootal, Mr F.E.O.	46091	Williams, William	
B-023	Home, Mr Thos.	6927	Holden, James	
B-024	Chabot, Mr David L.	13169	Grant, James	
B-025	Broderick-Cloete, Mr W.	46067	Holden, James	
B-026	Byington, Mr A. J.	46092	Grant, James	
B-027	Adams, Mr and Mrs Henry	1298	Holden, James	
B-028	Holt, Master Bobs	46130	Grant, James	
B-029	Turton, Mr Geo. H.	46120	Holden, James	
B-030	Gauntlett, Mr Fred. J.	46090	Grant, James	
B-030	Hopkins, Mr A.L.	46090	Grant, James	
B-031	Alles, Mr N.N.	46029	Holden, James	

Cabin No.	Name	Ticket No.	Steward	Notes
B-032	Chapman, Mrs W.	6924	Grant, James	
B-032	Morell, Mrs M.S.	6924	Grant, James	
B-033	Dredge, Mr and Mrs Alan	46134	Holden, James	
B-034	Williamson, Mr Chas F.	46059	Grant, James	
B-035	Seccombe, Mr Percy	1296	Holden, James	
B-036	Willey, Mrs Constance E.	20604	Grant, James	
B-037	Seccombe, Miss Elizabeth	1296	Holden, James	
B-038	Baker, Miss Marg't. A.	46059	Grant, James	
B-039	Lobb, Mrs Popham	46072	Holden, James	
B-040	van Straaten, Mr Martin	46060	Grant, James	
B-041	Turner, Mr Scott	46164	Holden, James	
B-042	Levinson, Mr Jos.	46163	Grant, James	
B-043	Campbell-Johnston, Mr and Mrs Conway S.	46147	Holden, James	
B-044	Jeffrey, Mr C.T.	20608	Grant, James	
B-045	Ratcliff, Mr Norman A.	46115	Holden, James	
B-046	Williams, Mr Thos H.	46140	Roach, John	
B-047 & bath	Allan, Lady	12933	Wood, Walter	
B-048 & bath	Bilicke, Mr and Mrs Albert C.	19841	Roach, John	
B-049 & bath	Allan, Miss Anna	12933	Wood, Walter	
B-049 & bath	Allan, Miss Gwen	12933	Wood, Walter	
B-050	Bowring, Mr Chas W.	46153	Roach, John	
B-051	Pearson, Dr and Mrs F.S.	46094	Wood, Walter	
B-052	Fowler, Mr and Mrs Chas F.	46078	Roach, John	
B-053	Young, Mr and Mrs J.M.	866	Wood, Walter	
B-054	Hickson Kennedy, Mrs C.	46138	Roach, John	
B-054	Hickson, Miss Katheryn	46138	Roach, John	
B-055	Vassar, Mr W.A.F.	46070	Wood, Walter	
B-056	Myers, Mr Herman A.	46089	Roach, John	
B-057	MacLennan, Mr F.E.	46168	Wood, Walter	
B-058	Pirie, Mr Robinson	46112	Roach, John	
B-059	Myers, Mr Joseph L.	46154	Wood, Walter	
B-060	Schwabacher, Mr Leo. M.	14346	Roach, John	
B-060	Sonneborne, Mr H.B.	14346	Roach, John	
B-061	Stainton, Mr William	46052	Wood, Walter	Mr Frohman's valet
B-062	Denyer, Mr Ronald	46032	Roach, John	Mr Vanderbilt's valet
B-062	Slingsby, Mr Geo.	1348	Roach, John	Mr Orr-Lewis's valet
B-063	Mills, Mr Chas V.	46039	Wood Walter	
B-064	Byrne, Mr Michael G.	46034	Roach, John	
B-065 B-067 & bath	Vanderbilt, Mr Alfred G.	46032	Wood, Walter	
B-066	Charles, Mr John H.	10858	Roach, John	
B-068 & bath	Thompson, Mr and Mrs E. Blish	46157	Roach, John	

Cabin No.	Name	Ticket No.	Steward	Notes
B-069	McMurray, Mr L.	10860	Wood, Walter	
B-070	Hubbard, Mr and Mrs Elbert	46096	Roach, John	
B-071	Peardon, Mr F.A.	13101	Wood, Walter	
B-072	Lockhart, Mr R.R.	10863	Roach, John	
B-073	Gorer, Mr Edgar	46057	Wood, Walter	
B-074	Orr-Lewis, Mr F.	1348	Roach, John	
B-075 & bath	Frohman, Mr Chas	46052	Collins, James	
B-076 & bath	Burnside, Miss Ives	13062	Clegg, Arthur	
B-076 & bath	Burnside, Mrs J.S.	13062	Clegg, Arthur	
B-077	Mason, Mr and Mrs Stewart S.	1295	Collins, James	
B-078	Pappadopoulo, Mr and Mrs M.N.	14673	Clegg, Arthur	
B-079	Davies, Emily	12933	Collins, James	Lady Allan's maid
B-079	Walker, Annie	12933	Collins, James	Miss Allan's maid
B-080	Waites, Mattie	13063	Clegg, Arthur	Mrs Burnside's maid
B-081	Bouteiller, Elsie	46061	Collins, James	Mrs Loney's maid
B-082	Hurley, Marg't	46123 / 46129	Clegg, Arthur	Mrs Learoyd's maid
B-083	Not occupied	n/a	n/a	
B-084	Not occupied	n/a	n/a	
B-085	Loney, Mr and Mrs A.D.	46061	Collins, James	
B-086 B-088 & bath	Thomas, Mr D.A.	46043	Clegg, Arthur	
B-087 & bath	Loney, Miss Virginia	46061	Collins, James	
B-089	Hammond, Mr and Mrs Fred'k	46128	Collins, James	
B-090	Mackworth, Lady	46045	Clegg, Arthur	
B-091	Hutchinson, Miss P.	46087	Collins, James	
B-092	Rhys-Evans, Mr A.L.	46044	Clegg, Arthur	
B-093	Kellett, Mr Francis C.	13191	Dawes, Thomas	
B-094	Matthews, Mr A.T.	13168	Penny, Percy	
B-095	Taylor, Mr R.L.	13165	Dawes, Thomas	
B-096	Sturdy, Mr Chas F.	13167	Penny, Percy	
B-097	Stewart, Mr Duncan	13166	Dawes, Thomas	
B-098	Shymer, Mrs R.D.	13092	Penny, Percy	
B-099	Paynter, Mr Chas E.	46133	Dawes, Thomas	
B-100	Kenan, Dr Owen	46143	Penny, Percy	Duplicate ticket numbers were issued to Dr Owen Kenan and Jessie Taft Smith.
B-101	Medbury, Mr M.B.	13093	Dawes, Thomas	
B-102	Wright, Mr Walter	46166	Penny, Percy	
B-103	Bernard, Mr Oliver	1299	Dawes, Thomas	
B-103	Morrison, Mr K.J.	46150	Dawes, Thomas	
B-104	Hardwick, Mr C.C.	46125	Penny, Percy	

Cabin No.	Name	Ticket No.	Steward	Notes
B-105	Paynter, Miss Irene	46133	Dawes, Thomas	
B-106	Brodrick, Mr C.T.	46135	Penny, Percy	Duplicate ticket numbers were issued to Mr C.T. Brodrick and Mr Frederico G. Padilla.
B-107	Crooks, Mr Robt W.	10865	Dawes, Thomas	
B-108	Friedenstein, Mr J.	46038	Penny, Percy	
B-109	Leigh, Mr Evan A.	6347	Dawes, Thomas	
B-110	Hill, Mr Chas T.	9956	Penny, Percy	
B-111	Colebrook, Mr H.G.	10866	Dawes, Thomas	
D-001	Dunsmuir, Mr Jas	10868	McLeod, William	
D-002	Forman, Mr Justin Miles	14469	Fletcher, William	
D-003	Clarke, Mr A.R.	13105	McLeod, William	
D-004	Daly, Mr H.M.	8498	Fletcher, William	
D-004	Freeman, Mr Rich'd R., Jr.	1390	Fletcher, William	
D-005	Oberlin, Miss Elise	13170	McLeod, William	Mrs Stephens's maid
D-005	Stephens, Mrs G.W.	13170	McLeod, William	
D-006	Harper, Mr John H.	46160	Fletcher, William	
D-007	Black, Mr Jas J.	46131	McLeod, William	
D-008	Padley, Mrs F.	46132	Fletcher, William	
D-009	Milton, Miss Caroline	13170	McLeod, William	John Stephens's nurse
D-009	Stephens, Master John H.C.	13170	McLeod, William	
D-010	Tesson, Mr and Mrs F.B	D1344	Fletcher, William	Duplicate ticket numbers were issued to Mr and Mrs Tesson and Mr Eugene Posen.
D-011	Fenwick, Mr John	46144	McLeod, William	
D-012	Clarke, Rev. Cowley	46062	Fletcher, William	
D-014	Charles, Miss Doris	13106	Fletcher, William	
D-015	Jolivet, Miss Rita	D1350	McLeod, William	
D-017	Watson, Mrs Wallace	13163	McLeod, William	
D-018	Dearbergh, Mr R.E.	46018	Fletcher, William	
D-020 & bath	Hammond, Mr and Mrs O.H.	46099	Fletcher, William	
D-021	Silva, Mr Thos. J.	46159	McLeod, William	
D-022	Dingwall, Mr C.A.	D1346	Fletcher, William	
D-023 & bath	Klein, Mr Charles	D1345	McLeod, William	
D-024	Tiberghien, Mr Geo.	46108	Fletcher William	
D-025	Bloomfield, Mr Thos.	46055	McLeod, William	
D-026	Lane, Sir Hugh	46101	Fletcher, William	
D-027	Bowers-Bartlett, Mr and Mrs G.W.	46104	McLeod, William	
D-028	Perry, Mr Fred'k J.	46152	Fletcher, William	
D-029	Jones, Miss Marg't D.	46093	McLeod, William	
D-029	Wakefield, Mrs A.T.	46093	McLeod, William	
D-030	Blandell, Miss Josephine	46031	Fletcher, William	
D-031	Campbell, Mr Alex.	46116	McLeod, William	Moved from D-039
D-032	Knight, Mr C. Harwood	14347	Fletcher, William	
D-033	Nyblom, Mr Gustav Adolph	46073	McLeod, William	

Cabin No.	Name	Ticket No.	Steward	Notes
D-034	Brown, Mr Wm. H.H.	D1349	Barnes, William	
D-035	Knight, Miss Elaine H.	14347	Huther, Edwin	
D-036	McConnell, Mr John W.	46014	Barnes, William	
D-037	Adams, Mr A.H.	46102	Huther, Edwin	
D-038	Perry, Mr Albert N.	46152	Barnes, William	
D-039	Grant, Mr and Mrs Montagu T.	26005	Huther, Edwin	Moved from D-031
D-040	Townley, Mr Ernest	13003	Barnes, William	
D-041	Drake, Mr Audley	46156	Huther, Edwin	Moved from A-005
D-042	Yung, Mr Philip	46066	Barnes, William	
D-043	Osbourne, Mrs T.O.	13430	Huther, Edwin	
D-044	Rogers, Mr Percy W.	6928	Barnes, William	
D-045	Adams, Mr Wm. McM.	46102	Huther, Edwin	
D-046	Walker, Mr David	46095	Barnes, William	
D-047	Posen, Mr Eugene Hy.	D1344	Huther, Edwin	Duplicate ticket numbers were issued to Mr Eugene Posen and Mr and Mrs Tesson.
D-048	Lehmann, Mr Isaac	46158	Barnes, William	
D-049	Maturin, Rev. Basil W.	46121	Huther, Edwin	
D-050	Powell, Mr Geo. A.	13064	Barnes, William	
D-051	Maurice, Mr Geo.	46105	Huther, Edwin	
D-052	Brown, Mrs M.C.	14311	Barnes, William	
D-052	Witherbee, Master A.S., Jr	14311	Barnes, William	
D-052	Witherbee, Mrs A.S.	14311	Barnes, William	
D-053	Shields, Mr and Mrs Victor E.	46145	Huther, Edwin	
D-054	Not occupied	n/a	Barnes, William	This cabin was originally occupied by Theodate Pope and her maid, Emily Robinson. They moved to cabin A-010.
D-055	Ryerson, Miss Laura	46106	Huther, Edwin	
D-055	Ryerson, Mrs G. Stanley	46106	Huther, Edwin	
D-056	Crompton, Mr and Mrs Paul	46081	Barnes, William	
D-057	Learoyd, Mr and Mrs C.A.	46123 / 46129	Huther, Edwin	
D-058	Crompton, Master Stephen	46081	Barnes, William	
D-058	Crompton, Master John	46081	Barnes, William	
D-059	McLean, Mr Walter	46149	Huther, Edwin	
D-059	McMurtry, Mr Fred'k	13061	Huther, Edwin	
D-060	Crompton, Miss Alberta	46081	Barnes, William	
D-060	Crompton, Miss Catherine	46081	Barnes, William	
D-060	Crompton, Romilly	46081	Barnes, William	
D-061	Luck, Master Eldridge C.	10541	Huther, Edwin	
D-061	Luck, Master Kenneth F.	10541	Huther, Edwin	
D-061	Luck, Mrs A.C.	10541	Huther, Edwin	
D-062	Allen, Miss Dorothy	46081	Barnes, William	Peter Crompton's nurse
D-062	Crompton, Master Peter	46081	Barnes, William	
D-063	Braithwaite, Miss Dorothy	12934	Huther, Edwin	
E-040	Pollard, Mr Henry	13133	Charlton, John	
E-041	Slidell, Mr Thos.	46127	Settle, Vincent	

Cabin No.	Name	Ticket No.	Steward	Notes
E-042	Strauss, Mr Julius	8677	Charlton, John	
E-043	Rankin, Mr Robt	46151	Settle, Vincent	
E-044	Perkins, Mr Edwin	46119	Charlton, John	
E-045	Macdona, Mrs Hy. D.	13047	Settle, Vincent	
E-046	Cross, Mr A.B.	46126	Charlton, John	
E-047	Friend, Mr Edwin W.	46083	Settle, Vincent	
E-048	Brooks, Mr J.H.	3080	Charlton, John	
E-049	Gilpin, Mr Geo. A.	46136	Settle, Vincent	
E-050	Fisher, Dr Howard	46111	Charlton, John	
E-051	Pearl, Major and Mrs F. Warren	46071	Settle, Vincent	
E-052	Mosley, Mr Geo. G.	46113	Charlton, John	
E-053	Mitchell, Mr Jas D.	11956	Settle, Vincent	A note in the berthing book states that, upon boarding, Mr Mitchell transferred to a different stateroom. The new cabin number is not given.
E-054	Watson, Mrs Anthony	14471	Charlton, John	
E-055	Stuart, Mr Alex.	13433	Settle, Vincent	
E-056	Bernard, Mr Chas P.	46155	Critchley, David	
E-057	Bistis, Mr Leonidas	46124	Wood, Alfred	
E-058	Grab, Mr Oscar F.	46161	Critchley, David	
E-059	Lines, Miss Alice	46071	Wood, Alfred	Nurse to the Pearl children
E-059	Pearl, Miss Amy W.W.	46071	Wood, Alfred	
E-059	Pearl, Miss Susan W.	46071	Wood, Alfred	
E-060	Sigurd, Mr Jacobus	1686	Critchley, David	
E-061	DePage, Mrs A.	46086	Wood, Alfred	
E-062	Vernon, Mr G.L.P.	D1347	Critchley, David	
E-063	Conner, Miss Dorothy	46111	Wood, Alfred	A note in the berthing book states that Miss Conner 'transferred to Dr Fisher.'
E-064	Hawkins, Mr F.W.	16050	Critchley, David	
E-064	Houghton, Dr J.T.	46167	Critchley, David	
E-065	Bohan, Mr Jas	13102	Wood, Alfred	
E-067	Lorenson, Miss Greta	46071	Wood, Alfred	Nurse to the Pearl children
E-067	Pearl, Master Stuart Duncan D.	46071	Wood, Alfred	
E-067	Pearl, Miss Audrey	46071	Wood, Alfred	In the berthing book, Audrey Pearl is listed simply as "Infant."
E-069	Bates, Mr Lindon, Jr.	46165	Wood, Alfred	
E-074	Osborne, Mrs A.B.	865	Critchley, David	
E-075	Copping, Mr and Mrs Geo. R.	13104	Wood, Alfred	
	Burgess, Mr Henry G.	13343	n/a	Purser to provide accommodation on board. Transfer from s.s. *Cameronia* May 1/15.
n/a	Cairns, Mr Robt W.	n/a	n/a	Purser to provide accommodation on board. To pay purser on board.
n/a	Winter, Mr	n/a	n/a	Purser to provide accommodation on board. Co.'s official.
n/a	Wright, Mr Robt C.	70416	n/a	Purser to provide accommodation on board. Transfer from s.s. *Cameronia* May 1/15.

Other titles published by Tempus

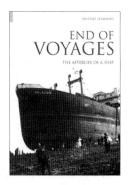

End of Voages The Afterlife of a Ship
MICHAEL STAMMERS

Looking at ships over the past two millennia, this is the first book ever to consider the question of 'what happens to a ship when it's no longer needed for its original purpose?' From Roman galleys to naval wooden walls, from the first liners to tugs and barges, and from ship-breaking to ship-wrecking, the whole history of shipping is considered in answering the question.

07524 3085 8

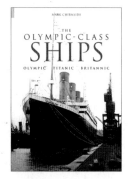

The Olympic-Class Ships Olympic Titanic Britannic
MARK CHIRNSIDE

In 1907, the owners of the White Star Line discussed their competition to the newly built Cunard liners, *Lusitania* and *Mauretania*, which resulted in designs of three superliners. *Olympic* and *Titanic* were to be built at Harland & Wolff's yard in Belfast, while the third ship, *Britannic*, was to follow after construction had been completed on the first pair of sisters. Illustrated with many rare images of all three vessels, only one of which survived in regular service, this is the definitive history of the most famous sister ships of all time.

07524 2868 3

RMS Olympic Titanic's Sister
MARK CHIRNSIDE

Mark Chirnside has written the first detailed history of the *Olympic* and here he tells the story of the ship and her time in service at war and in peace. With much previously unpublished information and illustrations, he explains why she was so important in terms of the development of the passenger ship. RMS *Olympic* simply was the most important ocean liner of her generation.

07524 3148 X

White Star Line
JANETTE MCCUTCHEON

White Star merged with Cunard in 1934 and the last liner, *Britannic*, was scrapped in 1960. Today, only the passenger tender, *Nomadic*, survives of this once great fleet. Janette McCutcheon tells the story of the White Star Line and their ships, using photographs and ephemera, transporting us back to a time of luxury travel that has gone forever.

07524 3147 1

If you are interested in purchasing other books published by Tempus, or in case you have difficulty finding any Tempus books in your local bookshop, you can also place orders directly through our website

www.tempus-publishing.com